The Pirates of Malabar

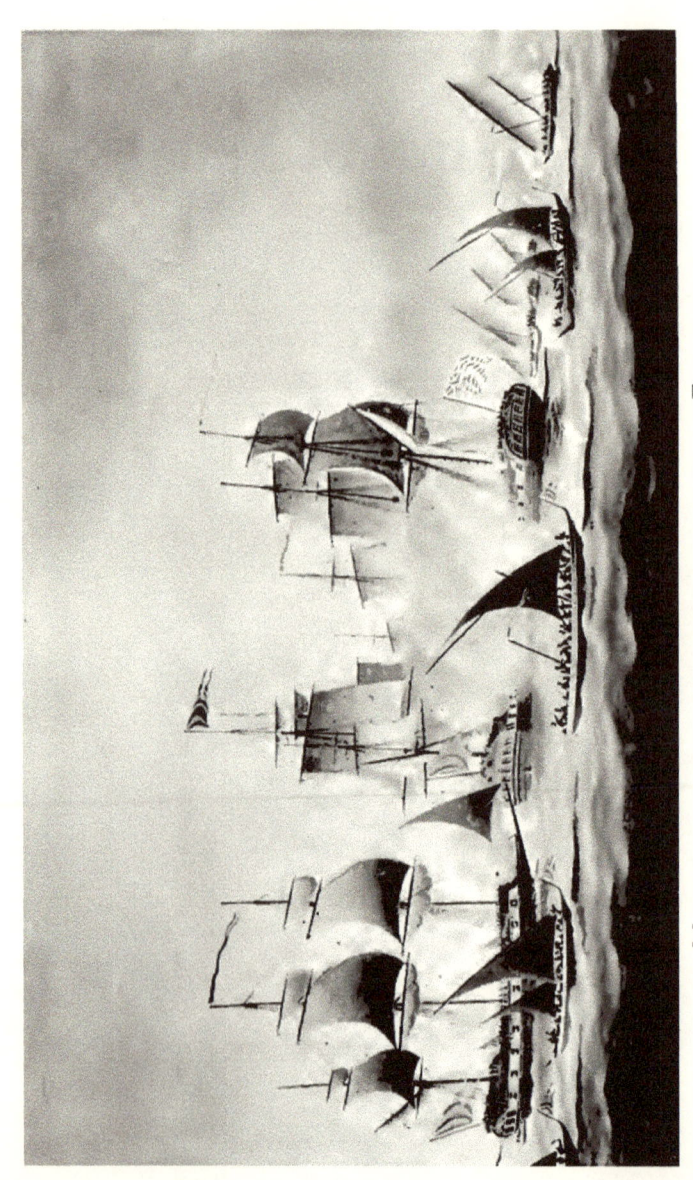

Mahratta *grabs* and *gallivats* attacking an English ship

The Pirates of Malabar
Pirates of the Coast of the Indian Sub-Continent
During the 17th & 18th Centuries

John Biddulph

The Pirates of Malabar
Pirates of the Coast of the Indian Sub-Continent During the 17th & 18th Centuries
by John Biddulph

First published under the title
The Pirates of Malabar
and
An Englishwoman in India Two Hundred Years Ago

Leonaur is an imprint of Oakpast Ltd
Copyright in this form © 2011 Oakpast Ltd

ISBN: 978-0-85706-753-1 (hardcover)
ISBN: 978-0-85706-754-8 (softcover)

http://www.leonaur.com

Publisher's Notes

The views expressed in this book are not necessarily those of the publisher.

Contents

Preface	7
Rise of European Piracy in the East	13
Captain Kidd	30
The Rise of Conajee Angria	44
An Active Governor	52
The Company's Servants	61
Expedition Against Kennery	70
Expedition Against Gheriah	76
Expedition Against Colaba	90
A Troubled Year in Bombay	104
Twenty-Six Years of Conflict	110
The Downfall of Angria	122
An Englishwoman in India Two Hundred Years Ago	135

Preface

For most people, interest in the doings of our forefathers in India dates from our wars with the French in the middle of the eighteenth century. Before then their lives are generally supposed to have been spent in monotonous trade dealings in pepper and calico, from which large profits were earned for their masters in England, while their principal excitements were derived from drinking and quarrelling among themselves. Little account has been taken of the tremendous risks and difficulties under which the trade was maintained, the losses that were suffered, and the dangers that were run by the Company's servants from the moment they left the English Channel. The privations and dangers of the voyage to India were alone sufficient to deter all but the hardiest spirits, and the debt we owe to those who, by painful effort, won a footing for our Indian trade, is deserving of more recognition than it has received. Scurvy, shortness of water, and mutinous crews were to be reckoned on in every voyage; navigation was not a science but a matter of rule and thumb, and shipwreck was frequent; while every coast was inhospitable.

Thus, on the 4th September, 1715, the *Nathaniel*, having sent a boat's crew on shore near Aden, in search of water, the men allowed themselves to be inveigled inland by treacherous natives, who fell upon them and murdered twelve out of fourteen who had landed from the ship. Such an occurrence now would be followed by a visit from a man-of-war to punish the murderers. Two hundred years ago it was only an incident to set down in the ship's log-book. But all such outrages and losses were small in comparison with those to which traders were exposed at the hands of pirates.

It is difficult to realize, in these days, what a terrible scourge piracy was to the Indian trade, two hundred years ago. From the moment of losing sight of the Lizard till the day of casting anchor in the port of destination an East India ship was never safe from attack, with the chance of slavery or a cruel death to crew and passengers, in case of capture. From Finisterre to Cape Verd the Moorish pirates made the seas unsafe, sometimes venturing into the mouth of the Channel to make a capture. Farther south, every watering-place on the African coast was infested by the English and French pirates who had their headquarters in the West Indies. From the Cape of Good Hope to the head of the Persian Gulf, from Cape Comorin to Sumatra, every coast was beset by English, French, Dutch, Danish, Portuguese, Arab, Malay or other local pirates. In the Bay of Bengal alone, piracy on a dangerous scale was practically unknown.

There was no peace on the ocean. The sea was a vast No Man's domain, where every man might take his prey. Law and order stopped short at low-water mark. The principle that traders might claim protection and vengeance for their wrongs from their country, had not yet been recognized, and they sailed the seas at their own risk. Before the close of the seventeenth century the buccaneers had passed away, but their depredations, in pursuit of what they called "free trade," were of a different nature from those of the pirates who succeeded them. Buccaneer exploits were confined to the Spanish main, where they ravaged and burnt Spanish settlements on the Atlantic and Pacific coasts, moving with large forces by sea and land.

According to Esquemeling, Morgan sailed on his expedition against Panama with thirty-seven sail and two thousand fighting men, besides mariners and boys. But the Spanish alone were the objects of their attack. So long as Spain claimed a monopoly of South American trade, it was the business of Spain alone to keep the marauders away; other Governments were not disposed to assist her. Hardly had the last of the buccaneers disappeared from the Western seas, when a more lawless race of rovers appeared, extending their operations into the Indian Ocean, acting generally in single ships, plundering vessels of every nationality, though seldom attacking places on shore.

Of these men, chiefly English, the most notorious were Teach, Every, Kidd, Roberts, England, and Tew; but there were many others less known to fame, who helped almost to extinguish trade between Europe, America, and the East. Some idea of the enormous losses caused by them may be gathered from the fact that Bartholomew Roberts alone was credited with the destruction of four hundred trading vessels in three years. In a single day he captured eleven vessels, English, French, and Portuguese, on the African coast.

War in Europe, and the financial exhaustion that ensued, rendered it almost impossible for the maritime powers to put an effective check on the pirates either in the East or the West. With peace their numbers increased by the conversion of privateersmen into freebooters. Slaver, privateers-man, and pirate were almost interchangeable terms. At a time when every main road in England was beset by highwaymen, travellers by sea were not likely to escape unmolested. But the chief cause of their immunity lay in the fact that it was the business of nobody in particular to act against them, while they were more or less made welcome in every undefended port.

They passed themselves off as merchantmen or slavers, though their real character was well known, but they paid royally for what they wanted; and, as gold, silver, and jewels were the principal booty from which they made their 'dividend,' many a rich bale of spices and merchandise went to purchase the good will of their friends on shore, who, in return, supplied their wants, and gave them timely information of rich prizes to be looked for, or armed ships to be avoided. They prided themselves on being men of honour in the way of trade; enemies to deceit, and only robbing in their own way. The Malabar coast was scandalized when Kidd broke the rule, and tricked or bullied people out of supplies. Officials high in authority winked at their doings from which they drew a profit, and when armed squadrons were sent to look for them, the commanders were not always averse to doing business with the freebooters.

The greatest sufferers among European traders in India were the English; for not only were the greater number of pirates of English blood, but pirate captains of other nationalities often sailed under English colours. The native officials, unable to distinguish the rogues from the honest traders, held the East India Company's servants responsible for the misdeeds of the *piccaroons*, from whom they suffered so grievously. Still, whatever their nationality might chance to be, it is fair to say that the generality of them were courageous rascals and splendid seamen, who, with their large crews, handled their ships better than any merchantmen could do.

When a pirate ship was cast away on a desolate coast, they built themselves another; the spirit of the sea was in their veins; whether building and rigging a ship, or sailing and fighting her, they could do everything that the most skilful seamen of the age could do. As was said half a century later of La Bourdonnais, himself a true *corsair* in spirit, their knowledge in mechanics rendered them capable of building a ship from the keel; their skill in navigation, of conducting her to any part of the globe; and their courage, of fighting against any equal force. Their lives were a continual alternation between idleness and extreme toil, riotous debauchery and great privation, prolonged monotony and days of great excitement and adventure.

At one moment they were revelling in unlimited rum, and gambling for handfuls of gold and diamonds; at another, half starving for food and reduced to a pint of water a day under a tropical sun. Yet the attractions of the life were so great that men of good position took to piracy. Thus, Major Stede Bonnet, of Barbados, master of a plentiful fortune, and a gentleman of good reputation, fitted out a sloop and went a-pirating, for which he was hanged, together with twenty-two of his crew, in November, 1718. Even women, like Anne Bonny and Mary Read, turned pirates and handled sword and pistol. Desperate, reckless, and lawless, they were filled with the spirit of adventure, and were the forerunners of the men that Hawke, Nelson, and Dundonald led to victory.

Long after they had disappeared from the seas the Indian trade continued to be exposed to the ravages of native pirates, who were not finally coerced into good behaviour till well into the nineteenth century. Of the European pirates Kidd, the most ignoble of them all, is alone remembered, while the name of Angria is only recalled in connection with the destruction of Gheriah by Watson and Clive. The long half-century of amateur warfare waged by Bombay against the Angrian power is dismissed in a few words by our Indian historians, and the expeditions sent forth by Boone against Angrian strongholds are passed over in silence. An account of some of them is given in Clement Downing's curious little book *Indian Wars*, valuable as the relation of an eye-witness; but the work, published in 1737, is inaccessible to the general reader, besides shewing many omissions and inaccuracies.

The early records of the East India Company have furnished the foundation on which this neglected chapter of our Indian history has been compiled. If the Company's servants appear at times in an unfavourable light, the conditions of their service must be considered, while the low standard of conduct prevailing in England two hundred years ago must not be forgotten. They were traders, not administrators, and the charter under which the Company traded was of very insecure duration. Twice the crown broke faith with them, and granted charters to rival associations. As the stability of the Company became assured, the conduct of its servants improved.

It is not intended in these pages to give an exhaustive account of all the pirates who haunted the Indian seas, but to present some idea of the perils that beset the Indian trade—perils that have so entirely passed away that their existence is forgotten.

Scattered among the monotonous records of the Company's trade are many touches of human interest. Along with the details relating to sugar, pepper, and shipping, personal matters affecting the Company's servants are set down; treating of their quarrels, their debts, and, too often, of their misconduct, as ordinary incidents in the general course of administration. At times a bright light is turned on some individual, who relapses into obscurity and is heard of no more, while the names of others emerge again and again, like a coloured thread woven in the canvas; showing how much romance there was in the lives of the early traders. One such thread I have followed in the account of Mrs. Gyfford, from her first arrival in India till her final disappearance in the Court of Chancery, showing the vicissitudes and dangers to which an Englishwoman in India was exposed two hundred years ago.

To Mr. William Foster, of the India Office, I am especially indebted for aid in directing my attention to old documents that would otherwise have escaped notice, and who has generously placed at my disposal some of the results of his own researches into the history of the Company in the seventeenth century, as yet unpublished.

My thanks are also due to Sir Ernest Robinson for permitting me to use his picture of an engagement with Mahratta ships, as a frontispiece.

J.B.

CHAPTER 1

Rise of European Piracy in the East

From the first days of European enterprise in the East, the coasts of India were regarded as a favourable field for filibusters, the earliest we hear of being Vincente Sodre, a companion of Vasco da Gama in his second voyage. Intercourse with heathens and idolaters was regulated according to a different code of ethics from that applied to intercourse with Christians. The authority of the Old Testament upheld slavery, and Africans were regarded more as cattle than human beings; while Asiatics were classed higher, but still as immeasurably inferior to Europeans. To prey upon Mahommedan ships was simply to pursue in other waters the chronic warfare carried on against Moors and Turks in the Mediterranean.

The same feelings that led the Spaniards to adopt the standard of the Cross in their conquest of Mexico and Peru were present, though less openly avowed, in the minds of the merchants and adventurers of all classes and nationalities who flocked into the Indian seas in the sixteenth and seventeenth centuries. With the decadence of buccaneering and the growth of Indian trade, there was a corresponding increase of piracy, and European traders ceased to enjoy immunity.

In 1623 the depredations of the Dutch brought the English into disgrace. Their warehouses at Surat were seized, and the president and factors were placed in irons, in which condition they remained seven months. This grievance was the greater, as it happened at the time that the cruel torture and execution of Captain Towerson and his crew by the Dutch took place at Amboyna. It was bad enough to be made responsible for the doings of their own countrymen, but to be punished for the misdeeds of their enemies was a bitter pill to swallow. In 1630, just as peace was being concluded with France and Spain, Charles I., who was beginning his experiment of absolute government, despatched the *Seahorse*, Captain Quail, to the Red Sea to capture the ships and goods of Spanish subjects, as well as of any other nations not in league and amity with England.

There were no Spaniards in the Red Sea or the Indian Ocean, but international arrangements in Europe were not regarded when the equator had been crossed. Quail captured a Malabar vessel, for which the Company's servants at Surat were forced to pay full compensation. The *Seahorse* returned to England in 1633, but in view of the new field of enterprise opened up, Endymion Porter, gentleman of the king's bedchamber, embarked on a piratical speculation, in partnership with two London merchants, Bonnell and Kynaston, with a licence under the privy seal to visit any part of the world and capture ships and goods of any state not in league and amity with England. Two ships, the *Samaritan* and *Roebuck*, were fitted out with such secrecy that the East India Company were kept in ignorance, and sailed in April, 1635, for the Red Sea, under Captain Cobb.

The *Samaritan* was wrecked in the Comoro Islands; but Cobb, continuing his cruise with the *Roebuck*, captured two Mogul vessels at the mouth of the Red Sea, from one of which he took a large sum of money and a quantity of goods, though the vessel had a pass from the Surat factory. Again the Company's servants at Surat were imprisoned, and not released till they had paid full compensation. Some small satisfaction was experienced when it became known that John Proud, master of the *Swan*, one of the Company's ships, had encountered the *Roebuck* in the Comoro Islands, and had attacked the freebooter. He was unable to capture it, but succeeded in procuring restitution of the captured goods; the treasure, however, was carried off to London, where it must have seemed as if the days of Drake and Hawkins had come again.

The Company laid their grievance before the king, who expressed much concern, promising to write to the Great Mogul and explain matters; so the Company commenced an action against Bonnell and Kynaston in the Admiralty Court. Porter was too highly placed to be struck at. Bonnell evaded arrest and escaped to France, but Kynaston was arrested and lodged in gaol; upon which Charles ordered his release on bail, saying he would try the case himself at his leisure.

But Porter's views went beyond a single piratical voyage. Hardly had Cobb started on his cruise, when he entered into partnership with Sir William Courten for an association to establish a separate trade to the East Indies. A royal grant was obtained, and the king himself was credited with a share to the nominal extent of £10,000. The grant was a flagrant breach of faith, and was the inauguration of the system of interlopers that in after years caused so much loss and trouble to the Company. Four ships were equipped and sent out, and before long it became known that two vessels from Surat and Diu had been plundered by Courten's ships, and their crews tortured. Again the Company's servants at Surat were seized and thrown into prison, where they were kept for two months, being only released on payment of Rs. 1,70,000, and on solemnly swearing to respect Mogul ships.

The Civil War brought these courtly piracies to an end, and the decay of the Spanish power drew the more turbulent spirits of Europe and America to the Spanish main, so that for a time there was a diminution of European piracy in Indian waters. As buccaneering became more dangerous, or less lucrative, adventurers of all nations again appeared in Eastern waters, and the old trouble reappeared in an aggravated form. The Indian Red Sea fleet offered an especially tempting booty to the rovers.

Lobo, a Jesuit priest, writing in the seventeenth century, tells us that so vast was the commerce of Jeddah, and so great the value of the ships trading to that place, that when, in India, it was wished to describe a thing of inestimable price, it was customary to say, 'It is of more value than a Jeddah ship.' Every year during the winter months, Indian traders, and pilgrims for Mecca, found their way in single ships to the Red Sea. On the setting in of the monsoon, they collected at Mocha, and made their way back in a single body. All Indian trade with the Red Sea was paid for in gold and silver, so that the returning ships offered many tempting prizes to freebooters.

In 1683 John Hand, master of the *Bristol*, interloper, cleared his ship with papers made out for Lisbon and Brazil, and sailed for Madeira. There he called his crew together, and told them he intended to take his ship to the East Indies. Those who were unwilling were overawed, Hand being a mighty 'pastionate' man. He appears to have been half pirate and half trader; equally ready to attack other traders, or to trade himself in spices and drugs. On the Sumatra coast, finding the natives unwilling to do business with him, he went ashore with a pistol in his pocket to bring the 'black dogs' to reason. The pistol went off in his pocket and shattered his thigh, and that was the end of John Hand.

In the same year, six men, of whom four were English and two Dutch, while on passage in a native merchant's ship from the Persian Gulf to Surat, seized the ship, killing the owner and his two wives. The lascars were thrown overboard, six being retained to work the ship. Their cruise did not last long. Making for Honore, they threw the six lascars overboard when nearing the port. The men managed to get to land, and reaching Honore, gave information of the would-be pirates to the local authorities, who seized the ship, and soon disposed of the rogues.

Three years later, two ships under English colours, mounting respectively forty-four and twenty guns, were reported to have captured vessels in the Red Sea, to the value of Rs.600,000. The *Seedee* of Jinjeera, who styled himself the Mogul's admiral, received a yearly subsidy of four *lakhs* for convoying the fleet, a duty that he was quite unable to perform against European *desperadoes*. Public opinion at Surat was at once excited against the English, and further inflamed by the Dutch and French, who were only too anxious to see a rival excluded from the trade. Sir John Child, to pacify the Governor, offered to send a man-of-war to look for the pirates; but the Dutch and French factors continued to 'spitt their venom' till the governor laughed in their faces and asked why they did not join in sending vessels to look for the rogues, since the matter seemed to them so serious.

In the same season a gallant engagement was fought against pirates, though not in Indian waters. The Company's ship *Caesar*, Captain Wright, bound from England for Bombay, was chased off the coast of Gambia by five ships, carrying each from twenty to thirty guns, under French colours. Wright had no intention of yielding without a struggle, so put his ship before the wind, to gain time for getting into fighting trim. The *Caesar* was carrying soldiers, and there were plenty of men to fight the ship. The boats were cut away, the decks cleared, ammunition and arms served out, three thousand pounds of bread which cumbered the gun-room were thrown overboard, and the tops were filled with marksmen.

As soon as all was ready, the mainsail was furled, and the ship kept under easy sail. Before long the two smaller ships came up, hoisted the red flag, and began firing, one on the *Caesar's* quarter and one astern. Soon the three other ships, two of which Wright styled the admiral and vice-admiral, came up. The admiral ranged up on the quarter and tried to board, but was obliged to sheer off, with the loss of many men and a bowsprit shot away. The vice-admiral tried to board at the bow, but with no better success, losing a foreyard and mizzen-mast. For five hours the engagement lasted, but the small-arm men in the *Caesar's* tops fired so well that the pirates could hardly serve their guns. The crew showed a wonderful spirits cheering loudly at every successful shot, till the discomfited pirates bore up, leaving the *Caesar* to pursue her way to Bombay, much knocked about as to hull, but having lost only one man killed and eight wounded.

In the following year came news to Surat of two vessels, under Danish colours, that had stopped English ships and seized native ones between Surat and Bombay. The *Phoenix*, a British man-of-war, was at Surat at the time, so, together with the *Kent*, East Indiaman, it was despatched to look after the marauders, taking with them also two small boys, sent to represent the French and the Dutch. In due time Captain Tyrrell returned, and reported that he had found a squadron of four vessels; that after a two days' chase he had brought them to, when they turned out to be two Danish ships, with two prizes they had taken. They showed him their commission, authorizing them to make reprisals on the Mogul's subjects for affronts offered to Danish traders; so he left them alone. A few months later the Portuguese factory at Cong, in the Persian Gulf, was plundered by an English pirate; another was heard of in the Red Sea, while Philip Babington an Irish pirate, was cruising off Tellichery in the *Charming Mary*.

By 1689 a number of sea rovers from the West Indies had made their appearance, and the factory at Fort St. George reported that the sea trade was 'pestered with pirates.' The first comers had contented themselves with plundering native ships. Now their operations were extended to European vessels not of their own nationality. In time this restriction ceased to be observed; they hoisted the red or black flag, with or without the colours of the nationality they affected, and spared no vessel they were strong enough to capture.

The Armenian merchants were loud in their complaints. An Armenian ship, bound from Goa to Madras, with twenty thousand pagodas on board, was taken by a pirate ship of two hundred tons, carrying twenty-two guns and a crew of sixty men. Another Armenian ship, with fifty thousand xeraphims, was taken near Bombay, on its voyage from Goa to Surat. Besides those that beset the Malabar coast, there were pirates in the Persian Gulf, at the mouth of the Red Sea, and in the Mozambique Channel, while five pirate vessels were cruising off Acheen. During the next ten years the losses caused by the pirates were prodigious.

Ovington mentions that at St. Helena (1689) they were told, by a slaver, of three pirates, two English and the other Dutch, so richly laden with booty that they could hardly navigate their ships, which had become weather-beaten and unseaworthy from their long cruises off the Red Sea mouth. Their worn-out canvas sails were replaced with double silk.

> They were prodigal in the expenses of their unjust gain, and quenched their thirst with Europe liquor at any rate this commander (the slaver) would put upon it; and were so frank both in distributing their goods, and guzzling down the noble wine, as if they were both wearied with the possession of their rapine, and willing to stifle all the melancholy reflections concerning it.

Such an account was bound to fire the imagination of every seaman who heard it.

The number of pirates was increased by the interlopers, merchant adventurers trading without a licence, who, like John Hand, when they failed to get cargoes, plundered native ships. Their proceedings were imitated by the permission ships, vessels that held the Company's licence for a single voyage. Not seldom the crews of interlopers and permission ships rose and seized the vessel against the will of their owners and commanders and hoisted the Jolly Roger. Commissions were granted to the East India Company's commanders to seize interlopers; but the interlopers, as a rule, were remarkably well able to take care of themselves. As pirates and interlopers alike sailed under English colours, the whole odium fell on the English.

In August, 1691, a ship belonging to the wealthy merchant, Abdul Guffoor, was taken at the mouth of the Surat River, with nine *lakhs* in hard cash on board. A guard was placed on the factory at Surat, and an embargo laid on English trade. As the pirate had shown the colours of several nationalities, the authorities were loath to proceed to extremities. Fortunately for the English Company, a member of the pirate crew was captured, and proved to be a Dane; so the embargo on English trade was taken off.

Though they plied their calling at sea, almost with impunity, the pirates occasionally fell victims to Oriental treachery on shore. Thus, James Gilliam, a rover, having put into Mungrole, on the Kattiawar coast, was made welcome and much praised for the noble lavishness with which he paid for supplies. Soon there came an invitation to a banquet, and Gilliam, with some of his officers and crew, twenty in all, were received by the representative of the *nawab* of Junaghur with excessive ceremony. Much polite curiosity was evinced about the noble strangers. "Why did they always go armed? Were their muskets loaded? Would they discharge them to show their host the European method?"

The muskets were discharged, and immediately the banquet was announced. "Delay to reload the muskets was inexpedient. It would be time to recharge their weapons after the feast." And then, when seated and defenceless, there was an irruption of armed men, and Gilliam, with his followers, were seized and fettered. For a year they lay at Junaghur, where two of them died. In vain Gilliam contrived to send a letter to the Surat factory, asking that they might be claimed as British subjects. President Harris knew that the least interest shown in the fate of the rovers would be fatal to the interests of the Company, and was relieved when he heard that they had been sent to Aurungzeeb's camp; after which they are heard of no more.

In the beginning of 1692, authority was given to the Company's commanders to seize pirates and hold them till the king's pleasure was known, but the measure was of small effect. The pirates were prime seamen, who outsailed and outfought the Company's ships; while among the Company's crews they had numerous sympathizers. The prizes to be gained were so great and the risks so small, that the Company could hardly restrain their own men from joining the sea rovers. Thus, in 1694, John Steel[1] ran away with the long boat of the *Ruby* frigate. Sixteen others who had plotted to join him were detected in time, and clapped in irons. The French and Dutch gave passes to all who applied for them, so Steel placed himself under French protection, and for two years 'that rogue Steel' finds frequent mention in the coast letters. Four years later Steel was arrested in England. But though the directors had been supplied with many accounts of his misdeeds, no sworn evidence could be produced against him, so Steel escaped scot-free.

All other pirates, however, were destined to be eclipsed in fame by Henry Every, *alias* Bridgman,[2] who now made his appearance in the Indian seas. His exploits, the great wealth he amassed by piracy, and his reputed marriage with a Mogul princess, continued to excite the public mind long after he had disappeared from the scene. Several biographies of him were written, one of them attributed to Defoe, all

---

1. It appears likely that this was the John Steel mentioned by Drury as his uncle in Bengal. There is very little doubt that much of Drury's alleged slavery in Madagascar was spent among the pirates.
2. It would appear that he assumed the name of Every on taking to piracy.

of them containing great exaggerations; and a play, *The Successful Pirate*, was written in his honour. His biographers generally give his name as John Avery, but it was as is here given.

According to the account of Van Broeck, a Dutchman, who was detained on board his ship for a time, and was on good terms with him, he was born at Plymouth, the son of a trading captain who had served in the navy under Blake. Every himself served in the navy, in the *Resolution* and *Edgar*, before he got the command of a merchant ship, in which he made several voyages to the West Indies. In May, 1694, he was first mate of the *Charles the Second*, one of the small squadron of English ships hired from Sir James Houblon, by the Spanish Government, to act against French smugglers who were troubling their Peruvian trade.[3]

The Spaniards were bad paymasters, and Houblon's squadron was detained at Corunna three or four months, while the crews became more and more discontented as their wages remained unpaid. As their sense of grievance increased, a plot was formed among the most turbulent spirits to seize a ship and turn rovers, under Every's command. On the night of the 30th May, the captain of the *Charles the Second* was made prisoner while in bed. A boat-load of men sent from the *James* to prevent the capture, joined the mutineers; the cables were cut, and the ship ran out of harbour. The captain and all who were unwilling to join were put into a boat, and the *Charles*, renamed the *Fancy*, was headed south for the coast of Africa. The only man detained against his will was the doctor, as he was a useful man.

Some months were spent on the Guinea coast, where some negroes were captured, and five ships—three English and two Danish—were plundered and burnt. Before the end of the year Every was east of the Cape, intent on the Red Sea traders. The first intelligence of him that reached Bombay was in May, 1695, when three outward-bound merchantmen reported that they had seen him at Johanna.

> Your Honour's ships going into that island gave him chase, but he was too nimble for them by much, having taken down a great deale of his upper works and made her exceeding snugg, which advantage being added to her well sailing before, causes her to sail so hard now, that she fears not who follows her. This ship will undoubtedly (go) into the Red Sea, which will pro-

---

[3]. Sir James Houblon was an Alderman of London, and a Governor of the Bank of England at the time.

cure infinite clamours at Surat.

Accompanying this report came the following characteristic letter from Every:—

> February ye 28th, 1695/4.
> To all English commanders lett this satisfye that I was riding here att this instant in ye ship *Fancy* man of *Warr* formerly the *Charles* of ye Spanish expedition who departed from Croniae ye 7th of May. 94: Being and am now in a ship of 46 guns 150 men & bound to seek our fortunes I have never as yett wronged any English or Dutch nor never intend whilst I am commander. Wherefore as I commonly speake with all ships I desire whoever comes to ye perusal of this to take this signall that if you or aney whome you may informe are desirous to know wat wee are att a distance then make your antient up in a ball or bundle and hoyst him att ye mizon peek ye mizon being furled I shall answere with ye same and never molest you: for my men are hungry stout and resolute: and should they exceed my desire I cannott help my selfe.
>
> as yett
> an Englishman's friend
> Henry Every.
>
> Here is 160 od French armed men now att Mohilla who waits for opportunity of getting aney ship, take care of your selves.[4]

According to Van Broeck, he was a man of good natural disposition, who had been soured by the bad treatment he received at the hands of his relations. The letter shows him to have been a man of some education, and during his short but active career in the Indian seas he appears to have attacked native ships only. The Company's records do not mention the loss of a single English ship at Every's hands, a circumstance that no doubt told heavily against the English in native opinion at Surat.

The same ships that brought Every's letter to Sir John Gayer brought intelligence of a well-known French pirate having got aground at Mohilla. The three Company's ships watering at Johanna, heard of the occurrence, and proceeded to the spot, burnt the French ship after taking out what treasure was on board, and captured six of

---

4. The letter appears to have been left by Every with the natives of Johanna, who gave it to the merchant captains who brought it to Bombay.

the Frenchmen, who were brought to Bombay. Every's friendly warning about the '160 od French armed men' evidently referred to the wrecked crew.

The value of Perim, or Bab's Key, as it was then called by mariners, to command the trade of the Red Sea, was at once perceived by Every, who attempted to make a settlement there. After some unprofitable digging for water, he abandoned the project, and established himself in Madagascar, which had before this become known as a pirate resort. During the next thirty years the only traders who dared show themselves on the Madagascar coast were those who did business with the pirates, owing to the number of pirate settlements that sprang up at different points; the best known being at St. Mary's Island, St. Augustine's, Port Dauphin, and Charnock's Point. They built themselves forts and established a reign of terror over the surrounding country, sometimes taking a part in native quarrels, and sometimes fighting among themselves; dubbing themselves kings, and living in squalid dignity with large seraglios of native women. Captain Woodes Rogers, who touched at Madagascar for slaves, sixteen years after Every's time, described those he met as having been on the islands above twenty-five years, with a motley crowd of children and grandchildren.

> Having been so many years upon this Island, it may be imagined their cloaths had long been worn out, so that their Majesties were extremely out at the elbows: I cannot say they were ragged, since they had no cloaths, they had nothing to cover them but the skins of beasts without any tanning, but with all the hair on, nor a shoe nor stocking, so they looked like the pictures of Hercules in the lion's skin; and being overgrown with beard, and hair upon their bodies, they appeared the most savage figures that a man's imagination can frame.[5]

One remarkable settlement was founded in the north, near Diego

---

[5]. The quotation is taken from Johnson's *History of the Pirates*. In his cruising voyage round the world Woodes Rogers did not touch at Madagascar. On that occasion (1711) he met two ex-pirates at the Cape, who had received pardons, and told him that the Madagascar settlements had dwindled to sixty or seventy men, "most of them very poor and despicable, even to the natives," and possessed of only one ship and a sloop. But, he adds, "if care be not taken, after a peace, to clear that island of them, and hinder others from joining them, it may be a temptation for loose straggling fellows to resort thither, and make it once more a troublesome nest of freebooters."

Life Aboard a British Privateer by Robert C. Leslie & Woodes Rogers also published by Leonaur.

Suarez, by Misson, a Frenchman, and the most humane of pirates, with whom was allied Tew, the English pirate. Misson's aim was to build a fortified town "that they might have some place to call their own; and a receptacle, when age and wounds had rendered them incapable of hardship, where they might enjoy the fruits of their labour and go to their graves in peace." The settlement was named Libertatia. Slavery was not permitted, and freed slaves were encouraged to settle there. The harbour was strongly fortified, as a Portuguese squadron that attacked them found to its cost. A dock was made; crops were sown; a Lord Conservator was appointed for three years, with a Parliament to make laws.

The colony was still in its infancy when it was surprised and destroyed by the natives, while Misson was away on a cruise; and so Libertatia came to an end. Tew succeeded in escaping to his sloop with a quantity of diamonds and gold in bars. On Misson rejoining him, they determined to go to America. Misson's ship foundered in a storm, while Tew made his way to Rhode Islands, and lived there for a time unquestioned. But the fascinations of a rover's life were too much for him. He fitted out a sloop and made again for the Red Sea, and was killed in action there with a Mogul ship.

From their Madagascar settlements the pirates scoured the east coast of Africa, the Indian Ocean as far as Sumatra, the mouth of the Red Sea, where the Mocha ships offered many rich prizes, the Malabar coast, and the Gulf of Oman. From time to time, ships from New England and the West Indies brought supplies and recruits, taking back those who were tired of the life, and who wished to enjoy their booty. European prisoners were seldom treated barbarously when there was no resistance, and the pirate crews found many recruits among captured merchantmen. Their worst cruelties were reserved for the native merchants of India who fell into their hands. They believed all native traders to be possessed of jewels, as was indeed often the case, and the cruellest tortures were inflicted on them to make them surrender their valuables.

One unhappy Englishman we hear of, Captain Sawbridge, who was taken by pirates, while on a voyage to Surat with a ship-load of Arab horses from Bombay. His complaints and expostulations were so annoying to his captors that, after repeatedly telling him to hold his tongue, they took a sail needle and twine and sewed his lips together. They kept him thus several hours, with his hands tied behind him, while they plundered his ship, which they afterwards set on fire, burning her and the horses in her. Sawbridge and his people were carried to Aden and set on shore, where he died soon after.

Before long. Every made some notable captures. Off Aden he found five pirate ships of English nationality, three of them from America, commanded by May, Farrell, and Wake. In the Gulf of Aden he burned the town of Mahet on the Somali coast because the people refused to trade with him. In September, while cruising off Socotra with the *Fancy*, two sloops, and a galley, he took the *Futteh Mahmood* with a valuable cargo, belonging to Abdool Quffoor, the wealthiest and most influential merchant in Surat. A few days later he took off Sanjan, north of Bombay, a ship belonging to the emperor, called the *Gunj Suwaie* (Exceeding Treasure).

This was the great capture that made Every famous. According to the legend, there was a granddaughter of Aurungzeeb on board, whom Every wedded by the help of a *moollah*, and carried off to Madagascar. But the story is only the most sensational of the many romantic inventions that have accumulated round Every's name. The native historian[6] who relates the capture of the *Gunj Suwaie*, and who had friends on board, would certainly not have refrained from mentioning such an event if it had occurred; nor would the Mogul emperor have failed to wreak vengeance on the English for such an insult to his family.

The *Gunj Suwaie* was the largest ship belonging to the port of Surat. It carried eighty guns and four hundred matchlocks, besides other warlike implements, and was deemed so strong that it disdained the help of a convoy. On this occasion it was returning from the Red Sea with the result of the season's trading, amounting to fifty-two *lakhs* of *rupees*[7] in silver and gold, and having on board a number of Mahommedan ladies returning from pilgrimage to Mecca.

In spite of the disparity of force, Every bore down and engaged. The first gun fired by the *Gunj Suwaie* burst, killing three or four men and wounding others. The main mast was badly damaged by Every's broadsides, and the *Fancy* ran alongside and boarded. This was the moment when a decent defence should have been made. The sailor's cutlass was a poor match for the curved sword and shield, so much so that the English were notorious in the East for their want of boldness in sword-play. But Ibrahim Khan, the captain, was a coward, and ran below at the sight of the white faces. His crew followed his example,

---

6. Elliot's *History of India* as told by its own historians. Muntakhabu-l Lubab of Khafi Khan.
7. Equal to £534,000 at that day.

and the vessel was taken almost without resistance.

So rich a prize was not to be relinquished without a very complete search. For a whole week the *Gunj Suwaie* was rummaged from stem to stern, while the crew of the *Fancy* indulged in a horrible orgy, excited beyond measure by the immense booty that had fallen into their hands. Several of the women threw themselves into the sea or slew themselves with daggers; the last piece of silver was sought out and carried on board the *Fancy*, the last jewel torn from the passengers and crew, and then the *Gunj Suwaie* was left to find its way to Surat as it best could.

The vials of long-accumulated wrath were poured out on the English. Instigated by Abdul Guffoor, the populace of Surat flew to arms to wreak vengeance on the factory. The governor, Itimad Khan, was well disposed to the English, but popular excitement ran so high that he found it difficult to protect them. Guards were placed on the factory to save it from plunder. A *mufti* urged that the English should be put to death in revenge for the death of so many true believers, and quoted an appropriate text from the *Koran*. Soon came an order from Aurungzeeb directing the *Seedee* to march on Bombay, and for all the English in Surat and Broach to be made prisoners. President Annesley and the rest, sixty-three in all, were placed in irons, and so remained eleven months. To make matters worse, news arrived of Every having captured the *Rampura*, a Cambay ship with a cargo valued at *Rs*.1,70,000.

> It is strange, (wrote Sir John Gayer), to see how almost all the merchants are incensed against our nation, reproaching the governor extremely for taking our part, and as strange to see that notwithstanding all, he stems the stream against them more than well could be imagined, considering his extreme timorous nature.

The strangeness of the merchants' hostility is hardly apparent, but it is not too much to say that Itimad Khan's friendly behaviour alone saved English trade from extinction. The Dutch, always hostile in the East, whatever might be the relations between Holland and England in Europe, strove to improve the occasion by fomenting popular excitement, and tried to get the English permanently excluded from the Indian trade. In the words of Sir John Grayer, "they retained their Edomitish principles, and rejoice to see Jacob laid low." But Itimad Khan knew that the pirates were of all nationalities, and refused to hold the English alone responsible. To propitiate the governor, Sir John Gayer made over to him the six French pirates taken at Mohilla, not without qualms at handing over Christians to Mahommedan mercies. He fully expected that the treasure taken out of the wreck would also be demanded of him; but Itimad Khan was not an avaricious man, and no such demand was made.

"His contempt of money is not to be paralleled by any of the King's Umbraws or Governors," Sir John wrote, a year later, when Itimad Khan was dead. To forestall the Dutch with the emperor, Gayer sent an agent offering to convoy the Red Sea fleet for the future, in return for a yearly payment of four *lakhs* a year. The offer was refused, but it served to place the English in a more favourable light, and to procure the cancelling of orders that had been given for attacking Bombay and Madras. Had it been accepted, the *Seedee* would have been added to the number of the Company's enemies. The Dutch, not to be outdone, offered to perform the same service in return for a monopoly of trade in the emperor's dominions. This brought all other Europeans into line against the Dutch proposal, and the intrigue was defeated.

The embargo on all European trade at Surat was maintained, while the Dutch, French, and English were directed to scour the seas and destroy the pirates. It was further ordered that Europeans on shore were not to carry arms or use *palanquins*, and their ships were forbidden to hoist their national flags. The Dutch and French hung back. They would not send a ship to sea without payment, except for their own affairs. Sir John Gayer, more wisely, sent armed ships to convoy the Mocha fleet, at the Company's charge, and so the storm passed off.

Meanwhile, Every, glutted with booty, made up his mind to retire[8] with his enormous gains. According to Johnson, he gave the slip, at night, to his consorts, sailed for Providence in the Bahamas, where his crew dispersed, and thence made his way to England, just at the time a royal proclamation offering £500 for his apprehension was published. The reward was doubled by an offer of four thousand *rupees* from the Company; eight *rupees* being the equivalent of a pound at that time.

---

8. According to the statement of a lascar, taken in the *Futteh Mahmood* and carried to Madagascar, Every sailed for the Bahamas in the autumn of 1695, so that his career in the Indian seas lasted only six months. On reaching Providence, Every presented the Governor with forty pieces of eight and four pieces of gold for allowing them to come and go in safety.

Several of his crew also straggled home and were captured; but before he left the Indian coast, twenty-five Frenchmen, fourteen Danes, and some English were put ashore, fearing to show themselves in Europe or America. This fact would seem to throw some doubt on the account of his having left his consorts by stealth.

On the 19th October, 1696, six of his crew were tried and sentenced at the Old Bailey, and a true bill was found and an indictment framed against Every himself, though he had not been apprehended. According to Johnson,[9] Every changed his name and lived unostentatiously, while trying to sell the jewels he had amassed. The merchant in whose hands he had placed them, suspecting how they had been come by, threatened him. Every fled to Ireland, leaving his jewels in the merchant's hands, and finally died in Devonshire in extreme poverty.

But the authority for this, as for most of the popular accounts of Every, is extremely doubtful. That he was cheated out of some of his ill-gotten gains is probable enough, but it is in the highest degree improbable that he was known to be living in poverty, and yet that the large reward offered for his apprehension was not earned. What is alone certain is that he was never apprehended, and that in a few months he carried off an amount of plunder such as never before was taken out of the Indian seas by a single rover. For long he was the hero of every seaport town in England and North America; innumerable legends gathered round his name, and an immense impulse was given to piracy.

A few months after his departure, there were five pirate ships in the Red Sea, under English colours; two more, each mounting fourteen guns, were in the Persian Gulf, and another was cruising off Tellicherry. At Madagascar others were coming in fast. The news of Every's great booty had spread from port to port, and every restless spirit was intent on seeking his fortune in this new Eldorado, as men nowadays flock to a new goldfield. The Company's sailors were not proof against the temptation. While on the way from Bombay to China the crew of the *Mocha* frigate mutinied, off the coast of Acheen, killed their captain, Edgecombe, and set afloat in the pinnace twenty-seven officers and men who refused to join them. The *Mocha* was then renamed the *Defence*, and for the next three years did an infinity of damage in the Indian Ocean.

At the same time, the crew of the *Josiah ketch* from Bombay, while

---

9. Johnson's *General History of the Pyrates*, 1724.

at anchor in the Madras roads, took advantage of the commander being on shore to run away with the ship. The whole thing had been planned between the two crews before leaving Bombay; their intention being to meet off the coast of Sumatra, and cruise in company. The piratical career of the *Josiah* did not last long. Making first for the Nicobars, the crew flocked on shore, and were soon involved in quarrels with the natives; leaving on board only two men, one of whom was James Cruffe, the armourer, who had been forced to join them against his will. The other man was but a lukewarm pirate, and Cruffe prevailed on him to join in an attempt to carry off the ship. They cut the cable, and by great good fortune, without any knowledge of navigation, succeeded in carrying the ship into Acheen.

Stout's command of the *Defence*, once *Mocha*, quickly came to an end. According to one account, he was put to death by his comrades, at the Laccadives, for trying to desert them; according to another account, he was slain by some Malays. His place was taken by Culliford, who had been the leader of the mutineers of the *Josiah*. He changed the ship's name to the *Resolution*, and proved himself one of the most daring rovers of his day.

The untrustworthiness of his crews placed Sir John Gayer in an awkward dilemma. He had to report to the directors that he dared not send ships to convoy pilgrims lest the crews should mutiny; that a boat could not be manned in Bombay harbour for fear of desertion, while, on shore, he had not a soldier fit to be made a corporal. A powerful French squadron had appeared on the coast, and the Surat President calculated that the Company's recent losses on captured ships sailing from Surat amounted to a million sterling. The losses of the native merchants were even more serious; trade was almost at a standstill, while three more pirate ships from New York appeared in the Gulf of Cambay, and captured country ships to the value of four *lakhs* of *rupees*. Every letter along the coast at this date speaks of the doings of the rovers: every ship coming into harbour told of pirates, of chases and narrow escapes, and of reported captures.

> These pirates spare none but take all they meet, and take the Europe men into their own ships, with such goods as they like, and sink the ships, sending the lascars on rafts to find the shore.
>
> So bold were the marauders that they cruised in sight of Bombay harbour, and careened their ships in sight of factories along the coast.

To avenge their losses, the Muscat Arabs, in April, 1697, seized the *London*, belonging to Mr. Affleck, a private merchant. The Arabs were engaged in hostilities with the Portuguese at the time, and forced the crew of the *London* to fight for them. Those who were unwilling were lashed to masts exposed to Portuguese fire, from which they did not escape scatheless. In vain the commanders of two of the Company's vessels assured the Imaum that the *London* was not a pirate.

> You have sent me a letter, (he wrote), about my people taking one of your ships. It is true that I have done so, in return for one you English took from me, so now we are even and have ship for ship; for this one I will not surrender. If you wish to be friends, I am willing to be so; if not, I will fight you and take all the ships I can.

One pirate ship was reported to have chased two Cong ships, capturing one and forcing the other ashore, where it became a total wreck. "What influence this may have on the Rt. Hon. Company's affairs, God alone knows," wrote the Surat President, mournfully. Soon he was in better spirits. The same pirates had landed and plundered Cong; but, allowing themselves to be surprised, fifty-six of the crew had been set upon and killed.

With few exceptions, the English pirates came from the American colonies. Every year, from New York, Boston, Jamaica, and the Bahamas, ships were fitted out, nominally for the slave trade, though it was no secret that they were intended for piracy in the Eastern seas. Whatever compunction might be felt at attacking European ships, there was none about plundering Asiatic merchants, where great booty was to be gained with little risk. Sometimes the governors were in league with the pirates, who paid them to wink at their doings. Those who were more honest had insufficient power to check the evil practices that were leniently, if not favourably, regarded by the colonial community, while their time was fully occupied in combating the factious opposition of the colonial legislatures, and in protective measures against the French and Indians.

The English government, absorbed in the French war, had no ships in the Indian seas; but the straits to which English trade in the East had been reduced, and the enormous losses caused by the pirates, at last forced some measures to be adopted for coping with the evil that had assumed such gigantic proportions.

CHAPTER 2

Captain Kidd

War with France was being actively prosecuted by land and sea. In 1695 the nation was still smarting under reverses in the Low Countries and the repulse of the Brest expedition. At sea the navy was holding its own, though English commerce suffered terribly under the attacks of French *corsairs* of Dunkirk and St. Malo. The Company applied for a ship to be sent to the Indian seas to deal with the pirates; but Lord Orford, the head of the Admiralty, refused to spare one. It was the fashion for wealthy men to obtain letters of marque for privateering, and a syndicate was formed, to which the Chancellor, Lord Somers, Lord Orford, Lord Bellamont, and other Whig nobles were parties, to send out a privateer against French commerce.

For this purpose the *Adventure* galley was purchased and fitted out, and the command was given to William Kidd, who was suggested to Lord Bellamont as a fit person for the task. Kidd was an old privateers-man who had gained some reputation in the West Indies during the war. Lord Bellamont had been appointed Governor of New York, though he did not proceed there till two years later. The king had charged him to use his utmost endeavours to put a check on the pirates who sailed from New England, and nothing better occurred to him than to obtain a commission for Kidd to act against the rovers. A general reward of £50 was offered for the apprehension of each pirate, and £100 for Every, increased in the following year to £500.

In December, a commission under the Admiralty Seal was issued to Kidd, authorizing him to proceed against French shipping. He was to keep a journal of his proceedings, and any ship captured was to be carried into the nearest port and legally adjudged by a competent court. If condemned, he might dispose of it according to custom. Six weeks later, a second commission under the Great Seal was granted him, in his capacity of a private man of war, to apprehend all pirates, freebooters, and sea rovers, the names of Thomas Too (? Tew), John Ireland, Thomas Wake, and William Maze, or Mace, being specially mentioned.

Again, he was enjoined to keep an exact journal of his doings, and the pirate ships he captured were to be proceeded against according to law, in the same manner as French captures. A subsequent warrant was granted to the syndicate, who figure in it as the Earl of Bellamont, Edmund Harrison, William Rowley, George Watson, Thomas Reynolds, and Samuel Newton. Under these unpretentious names were hidden Lords Orford and Somers, and other Whig nobles. They were to account for all goods and valuables captured in the rovers' possession: one-tenth was to be reserved for the Crown, the rest being assigned to them to recoup their expenditure.

The *Adventure* carried thirty guns and rowed twenty-six or thirty oars. In May, 1696, Kidd sailed from Plymouth for New York with a crew of about seventy men. On the way he captured a small French vessel, which was properly condemned, and the proceeds helped to complete the equipment of the *Adventure*. In New York he filled up his crew to one hundred and fifty-five men, and people shook their heads when they saw the men of doubtful character that he enlisted. It was felt at the time that, either his intentions were dishonest, or he was taking a crew that he would be unable to control. The men were promised shares of what should be taken, while Kidd himself was to have forty shares. Nothing was said as to the share of the owners or the Crown. In September he sailed for the Cape. There were plenty of pirates and French trading-ships close at hand on the American coast, but he did not waste a day in looking for them.

Within a few days of Kidd's leaving Plymouth, a royal squadron consisting of the *Windsor, Tyger, Advice*, and *Vulture*, under Commodore Warren, sailed from Sheerness to visit the harbours and wateringplaces, used by East India ships, as far as the Cape, and clear them of pirates. The squadron, with five East Indiamen under convoy, made its way slowly along the African coast, losing many men from sickness. Two hundred leagues west of the Cape they sighted a strange sail that seemed to wish to avoid them. Warren gave chase and forced it to heave to.

On being signalled to come on board, the commander proved to be Kidd, in command of the *Adventure*. Asked to account for himself, he told how he was engaged to look for Every and destroy pirates, and showed his commission. Apparently, this was the first that Warren had heard of him, but there was no gainsaying the royal commission, so the usual hospitality was shown him, and he was bidden to keep company as far as the Cape. Warren had lost many men on the Guinea coast, and asked Kidd to spare him some. No better opportunity could have been found for getting rid of troublesome men, but Kidd declined to part with a single one.

As Warren's wine told on him, his true character showed itself. He boasted of the feats he was going to do, and the wealth he would get, till Warren was filled with disgust and suspicion. The *Adventure* wanted a new mainsail. Warren could not spare him one. No matter, he would take one from the first ship he met; and he was finally sent back to the *Adventure*, reeling drunk. For six days he sailed in company with the squadron. Then a calm came on, and at night, making use of his oars, Kidd stole away, and was nearly out of sight when the sun rose.

On reaching the Cape, Warren could get no news of him, but to the captains of the Company's ships he communicated his suspicions of Kidd. Three of them, bound for Johanna in the Comoro Islands, the *Sidney*, the *Madras Merchant*, and the *East India Merchant*, agreed to sail in company for mutual protection. The *Sidney*, being the faster sailer, reached Johanna in advance of her consorts, and found the *Adventure* at anchor in the roadstead. As the *Sidney* came to anchor, Kidd sent a boat to Captain Gyfford, ordering him to strike his colours, and threatening to board him if he refused. Gyfford prepared to defend himself. Two days later the *East India Merchant* and the *Madras Merchant* appeared, making for the anchorage, and Kidd lowered his tone. He then invited the three captains to come on board the *Adventure*, which they refused to do, letting him plainly see that they distrusted him.

Soon they had to warn him regarding his ill-treatment of the Johanna people, for which they threatened to call him to account. This unlooked-for attitude on the part of the three captains made Kidd uneasy; and finding that they would not leave the anchorage till he had gone, he made sail and departed. Some of the crew of the *Adventure* had, however, used suspicious language, saying they were looking for an East India ship. When asked if they would attack a single one, they answered evasively, while continuing to boast of the things they were going to do.

These early proceedings of Kidd effectually dispose of the plea that his intentions were at first honest, and that he only yielded to the coercion of his crew in taking to piracy, after reaching the Indian seas.

The truth is that Kidd was resolved on piracy from the first, and had little difficulty in persuading the majority of the crew to join him. It can hardly be doubted that the accounts of the great wealth acquired by Every had turned his head. There were a number of men on board the *Adventure* who were unwillingly coerced into piracy, and who remained in a chronic state of discontent, but Kidd was not one of them. Long before he had made a single capture, it was reported in the ports of Western India that Kidd was a pirate.

From Johanna he shaped his coarse for Madagascar, but the pirates were all away in search of prey; so he continued his cruise in the Mozambique Channel and along the African coast. He is said to have met Indian ships at this time without molesting them, which was afterwards cited to show that his intentions were then honest. It is more likely that he was only doubtful as to his own power, being unacquainted with the weakness of Asiatics, and reserving himself for the rich prey offered by the Mocha fleet.

Cruising northwards, he landed at Mabber[1] on the Somali coast, and took some corn from the natives by force—his first bit of filibustering. Then making for Perim, he anchored to await the Mocha fleet. Three times he sent a boat to look into Mocha harbour, and bring notice when the Indian ships were ready to sail. As the fleet in scattered array emerged from the straits, he singled out a large vessel and began firing at it. This at once attracted the attention of the *Sceptre* frigate that Sir John Gayer had sent as a convoy, and Kidd took to his heels.

If Every had been in his place, he would have followed the fleet across the Indian Ocean, and have picked up a straggler or two, but the sight of the *Sceptre* and a Dutch man-of-war had been enough for Kidd, and he left the pilgrim fleet alone. Without molesting them further, he made his way eastward, and, on the 29th August, off Sanjan, north of Bombay, he took the *Mary* brigantine, a small native vessel from Surat. This was Kidd's first capture on the high seas. Thomas Parker, the master of the *Mary*, was forced on board the *Adventure* to act as pilot, a Portuguese was taken to act as interpreter, and the lascars of the *Mary* beaten and ill-treated.

A week later he put into Carwar for provisions, flying English colours; but his character was already known. The Sunda Rajah and the factory stood on their guard while he was in harbour. Harvey, the chief of the factory, demanded the surrender of Parker, but Kidd

---

1. This was probably a village near Ras Mabber, about one hundred and sixty-five miles south of Cape Guardafui.

vowed he knew nothing about him. Eight of his crew deserted, and told their story. They had no desire for the piratical life into which they had been trepanned, and reported that many more of the crew would leave him if they could get the chance. While off Carwar he careened the *Adventure* on a small islet in the harbour, which was long known as Kidd's island. A month later he was off Calicut, where his ever-recurring trouble about supplies is shown in the following letter to the factory:—

Adventure Gally, October ye 4't, 1697.

Sir,

I can't but admire yet your people is so fearfull to come near us for I have used all possible means to let them understand yet I am an Englishman and a ffreind not offering to molest any of their cannoes so think it convenient to write this yet you may understand whome I am which (I) hope may end all suspition. I come from England about 15 mos. agone with y'e King's Commission to take all pyrates in these seas, and from Carwar came about a month agone, so do believe yet (you) have heard whome I am before yet and all I come for here is wood and water which if you will be pleased to order me shall honestly satisfie for ye same or anything that they'l bring off which is all from him who will be very ready to serve you in what lyeth in my power.

William Kidd.

They knew who he was only too well, so he sailed for the Laccadives, whence news was soon received of his barbarous treatment of the natives, and that he had killed his quartermaster.[2] The letter is characteristic of Kidd's methods. From his first entrance into the Indian seas his conduct had aroused suspicion. Owing to the large amount of coasting trade and the frequent necessity of calling at many places for water, the news of the sea spread from port to port with great rapidity. At the moment of his writing this letter he had the master of the *Mary* a prisoner under hatches, and the factory chiefs of Carwar and Calicut were well aware of it; but to the end he believed that he could throw dust in the eyes of the Company's officials by making

---

2. In ships of this class the quartermaster was next in importance to the captain or master. The incident refers to the death of Moore, the gunner of the *Adventure*, who was killed by Kidd in a fit of anger for saying that Kidd had ruined them all. The killing of Moore was one of the indictments against Kidd at his trial.

play with the royal commission.

While he was on the coast, Kidd was chased by two Portuguese armed vessels, a *grab* and a sloop. The *grab* was a poor sailer, and Kidd had no difficulty in eluding it; but the sloop, a better sailer, allowed itself to be drawn on in chase, till Kidd, shortening sail, was able to give it several broadsides, which reduced it to a total wreck; after which he showed a clean pair of heels. At Kidd's trial it was stated he had ten men wounded in this business.

In April (1698) the *Sedgwick*, arriving at Fort St. David, reported that on its way from Anjengo it had been chased for three days and nights by Kidd, but had been saved by a stiff breeze springing up. On its return voyage the *Sedgwick* was less fortunate, being captured off Cape Comorin by Chivers, a Dutchman, in the *Soldado*, otherwise known as the *Algerine*, of two hundred and fifty tons and carrying twenty-eight guns. The cargo of the *Sedgwick* not being to Chivers' liking, and being put into good humour with sundry bowls of punch, he let the *Sedgwick* go, taking out of her only sails and cordage.

The year 1698 saw the Company's trade almost extinguished owing to the depredations of the sea rovers and the hostility aroused against Europeans. Every letter brought accounts of the pirates and the losses occasioned by them. In small squadrons they swept the coast from Madras to the mouths of the Indus, and haunted the sea from Cape Comorin to the Straits of Malacca. In July, the Company's ship *Dorrill*, bound for China, was attacked in the Straits of Malacca by the *Resolution*, late *Mocha*, commanded by Culliford, and, after a hot engagement of three hours, made the pirate sheer off, with heavy losses on both sides. Bowen in the *Speedy Return*, for the taking of which Green was, with doubtful justice, hanged, Chivers in the *Soldado*, North in the *Pelican*, Halsey, Williams, White, and many others of less fame, were plundering and burning everywhere with impunity.

Early in the year, Kidd captured the *Quedah Merchant* a country ship bound from Bengal to Surat, belonging to some Armenian merchants who were on board. The captain was an Englishman named Wright; the gunner was a Frenchman, and there were two Dutchmen. This was the best prize made by Kidd, and yielded some £10,000 or £12,000, which was at once divided among the crew of the *Adventure*, Kidd's forty shares being one-fourth of the whole. Able seamen got one share; landsmen and servants a half-share only. The Surat factory was filled with alarm, not without good reason. In vain Sir John Gayer wrote to the governor, and sent an agent to the emperor to disclaim responsibility.

In August came an imperial order directing that the English, French, and Dutch should be held responsible for all losses, and that for the *Quedah Merchant* alone the English should pay two *lakhs* of *rupees*. Guards were placed on the factories; all communication with them was forbidden; their Mahommedan servants left them, and their creditors were made to give an account to the governor of all debts owing by Europeans. The Dutch and French tried to exonerate themselves by laying all the blame on the English, but the governor refused to make any distinction, and called on the three nations to pay fourteen *lakhs* of *rupees* as a compensation for the losses occasioned by piracy.

Sir John Gayer was a man of action. Like Macrae, to be mentioned later in these pages, he had first brought himself into notice as a sea-captain, and as governor of Bombay had upheld the Company's interests for four years, in circumstances of no ordinary difficulty. The time for some decided action had arrived if the Company's trade was to continue. On receiving intelligence of these occurrences, he appeared off Surat with three armedships, and sent word to the governor that he would neither pay any portion of the fourteen *lakhs*, nor give security. At the same time he intimated that he was ready to furnish convoys for the Mocha ships, as he had already done, and, in proof of good will in acting against the pirates, pointed out that, now the war in Europe was at an end, a royal squadron was on its way to the Indian seas to extirpate them.

The European traders on the west coast had always been so submissive to the emperor's authority that this unexpected display of vigour astonished the governor: he moderated his tone. The Dutch declared they would abandon the Surat trade rather than pay; so the governor consented to make no demand for past losses, if the English would engage to make good all future losses by piracy. This was also refused. Finally, the English, French, and Dutch agreed to act in concert to suppress piracy, and signed bonds by which they jointly engaged to make good all future losses.

Onerous as these terms were, the agreement came not a moment too soon. The news of it reached Aurungzeeb just in time to procure the reversal of an order he had issued, putting a final stop to all European trade in his dominions. He told the Surat governor to settle the matter in his own way. In pursuance of the agreement, the Dutch convoyed the Mecca pilgrims and patrolled the entrance to the Red Sea, besides making a payment of *Rs.*70,000 to the governor; the English paid *Rs*.30,000 and patrolled the South Indian seas; while the French made a similar payment and policed the Persian Gulf.

An experience of the *Benjamin* yacht at this time showed that pirates were not prone to wanton mischief, where there was no plunder to be gained. In November, the yacht lay at Honore, taking in a cargo of pepper, when the well-known pirate ships *Pelican, Soldado,* and *Resolution* came into harbour for provisions. Seeing the Bombay governor's yacht, they naturally concluded that some attempt would be made to prevent the natives from supplying their wants. They at once sent word to the master of the *Benjamin* that they had no intention of molesting him, unless he hindered them in getting provisions, in which case they would sink him. The master of the yacht was only too glad to be left alone; the pirates got their provisions, and, in recognition of his behaviour, presented him with a recently captured Portuguese ship. Sir John Gayer, in much fear lest he should be accused of being in league with the pirates, quickly made it over to the Portuguese authorities.

When the intelligence of Kidd's piracies reached England, there was a storm of indignation in the country. Party feeling was running high and with unusual violence. The majority in the House of Commons desired the ruin of Somers and Orford while aiming at the King. The charge of abetment in Kidd's misdeeds was too useful a weapon to be neglected, so it was added to the list of accusations against them. It must be admitted that the circumstances of the Lord Chancellor, the head of the Admiralty, and other prominent men using their influence to forward a venture from which they were to profit, under fictitious names, and that had created such a scandal, demanded inquiry. It was hardly sufficient to say that they had lost their money. Such an answer would justify any illegal enterprise in the event of its failure.

The French war had come to an end, so in January, 1699, a royal squadron of four men-of-war, the *Anglesea, Harwich, Hastings,* and *Lizard,* sailed from Portsmouth for Madagascar under Warren.[3] They carried with them four royal commissioners and a proclamation offering a free pardon, from which Every and Kidd were excepted, to all pirates who voluntarily surrendered themselves before the end of April, 1699. The pardon related only to acts of piracy committed east of the Cape of Good Hope, between the African and Indian coasts. After calling at St. Augustine's bay, where several pirates made their submission, the squadron reached Tellicherry in November.

---
3. Warren had returned from his first cruise in the autumn of 1697.

As it came to its anchorage, Warren died, and was buried on shore the following day. He was succeeded in the command by Littleton. In the following May, Littleton was on the Madagascar coast, where he remained till the end of the year before returning home. During the whole time he was in communication with the pirates. His dealings with them brought him into disrepute in shipping circles. Hamilton tells us that "for *some valuable reasons* he let them go again; and because they found a difficulty in cleaning the bottoms of their large ships, he generously assisted them with large blocks and tackle falls for careening them." Possibly Hamilton's remark was due to the conduct of Captain White of the *Hastings*, whose behaviour excited such suspicion that Littleton placed him under arrest, fearing he would make his ship over to the pirates.

Littleton remained on the Madagascar coast for eight months without firing a shot. When he first reached St. Mary's, the pirates greeted him with a salute of nine guns, to which he responded with five, and he was in close and daily communication with them. Whether any pirates made their submission to him does not appear; but it is probable that his presence strengthened the resolution to obtain pardon of those who had previously engaged themselves to Warren; among them Culliford and Chivers. The fact is that piracy was looked upon then more leniently than we should now regard it. Plundering and ill-treating Asiatics was a venial offence, and many a seaman after a cruise with the pirates returned to his calling on board an honest merchantman, without being thought much the worse for it.

Among all the naval officers sent to the Indian seas at that time, Warren appears to have been the only one who really tried to protect the Company's interests. Littleton quarrelled with Sir Nicholas Waite, and had questionable dealings with the Madagascar pirates. Richards and Harland quarrelled with Sir John Gayer, and crippled the Company's ships by forcibly pressing their sailors to fill up their own crews; while Matthews exceeded them all in outrageous behaviour, as will be recounted in its place.

After capturing the *Quedah Merchant*, Kidd shaped his course for Madagascar, where he found Culliford in the *Resolution*, who at first treated him with suspicion, hearing that he had a commission to capture pirates. But Kidd soon reassured him over sundry cups of bombo, protesting with many oaths that 'his soul should fry in hell' sooner than that he should hurt a hair of one of Culliford's crew; and, as a proof of good will, presented him with two guns and an anchor. Then, finding the *Adventure* had become unseaworthy, he abandoned her, and sailed for New England in the *Quedah Merchant*. In June, 1799, he reached Boston.

Before his arrival, he heard he had been proclaimed a pirate, so he deputed a friend to approach Lord Bellamont on his behalf. The *Quedah Merchant* was disposed of, and his plunder placed in a safe place. By assurance, and by a valuable present to Lady Bellamont, he thought he could face matters out. Bellamont appears to have been puzzled at first how to treat him. He was unwilling to believe all that was said. At the end of three weeks he made up his mind and arrested Kidd. For eight months he lay in Boston gaol, and was then sent to London for trial, remaining in Newgate for more than a year. Eleven of his crew were also arrested, two of them being admitted as King's witnesses.

In the interval the storm against the Whig ministers had gathered strength, and articles of impeachment against Somers, Orford, and others were being prepared by the House of Commons. On the 27th March, 1701, Kidd was brought to the House to be examined, but he said nothing to inculpate any of the owners of the *Adventure*, so a resolution was passed that he should be proceeded against according to law.

On the 8th and 9th May he was brought up for trial at the Old Bailey. The first indictment against him was for the murder of Moore, the gunner of the *Adventure*. There had been a quarrel in which Moore accused Kidd of having ruined them all, on which Kidd called him a 'lousy dog'; to which Moore replied in a rage, that if he was a dog it was Kidd who had made him one. At this Kidd hurled a bucket at him and fractured his skull. The jury found him guilty. He was then tried, together with nine of his crew, for the taking of the *Quedah Merchant*. His line of defence was that it was sailing under a French pass, and therefore a lawful prize, but he evaded actually saying so. He declared that Lord Bellamont had some French passes of ships he had taken, but would not produce them.

That Kidd had captured some ships under French passes, and that the passes were in Bellamont's hands, is extremely probable; but it is incredible that a French pass for the *Quedah Merchant* was in Bellamont's hands, and that he held it back. He had been accused of complicity in Kidd's piracies, and threatened with impeachment. Every consideration of private and political interest alike prompted him to clear himself of the charge, and confound those who accused the leading men of his party as well as himself.

Kidd tried to get the witnesses, some of them favourable to him, to say they had seen the French pass, but all they could say was that they had heard him declare there was one. The adverse witnesses deposed that he had feigned to believe that the French gunner of the *Quedah Merchant* was the captain, though they all knew he was not. When asked, "Captain Kidd, can you make it appear there was a French pass aboard the *Quedah Merchant*?" he replied, "My lord, these men say they heard several say so."

One of the Armenian owners was in court, but he did not examine him; nor could he say why he had not had the ship properly condemned, like the French ship taken between Plymouth and New York. His only reply was that he was not at the sharing of the goods, and knew nothing of it. For his attack on the Mocha fleet he offered no explanation.

He was found guilty, and was then tried for the captures of a Moorish ship (Parker's), a Moorish *ketch*, and a Portuguese ship. Culliford and two others were next tried for taking a ship called the *Great Mahomet*. Three of Kidd's crew were acquitted, the rest of the prisoners were found guilty, and sentenced to be hanged. Culliford was respited, having made his submission to Warren. Three of Kidd's crew had hard measure dealt to them. They had made their submission under the King's proclamation, but not to one of the commissioners appointed for the purpose, so their submission went for nothing. On the 12th May, Kidd, with six of his crew and two of Culliford's, was hanged at Execution Dock, the common place of execution for pirates.

It is impossible to follow Kidd's career, and to study his trial, without coming to the conclusion that he deserved his fate. There is no sign that he was sacrificed to political expediency. Directly the House of Commons failed to bring home the responsibility for Kidd's piracies to the leaders of the Whig party, he ceased to be of any importance for political purposes. The charge of complicity with him was only one of ten charges against Orford, one of fourteen against Somers. The court is said to have dealt hardly with him, but courts of justice were not very tender to any criminals in those days, and the jury did not hesitate to acquit three of those tried with him.

Criminals were not allowed the aid of counsel, except on a point of law. Kidd did raise a legal point, and was allowed the aid of a counsel to argue it. His intention was clear from the day he left New York. The four pirates named in his commission were then on the American coast; he made no effort to look for them, but steered at once for the

Cape. If he could not control his crew, he could have invoked Warren's help; instead of which he stole away in the night. His threats to the *Sidney* at Johanna, his attack, after three weeks' waiting, on the Mocha fleet, his detention of Parker, to say nothing of his dealings with Culliford, can only be interpreted in one way. During his whole cruise he never put into Surat, Bombay, or Goa, but cruised like any other pirate.

The legend of his buried treasure has survived to our own day, owing to the fact that he had buried some of his booty before putting himself in Bellamont's hands; but the record of his trial shows that, beyond what was obtained from the *Quedah Merchant*, his plunder consisted mostly of merchandise. That some of his ill-gotten gains were recovered at the time seems clear from an Act of Parliament passed in 1705, enabling the crown to "dispose of the effects of William Kidd, a notorious pirate, to the use of Greenwich Hospital"; which institution received accordingly 6472-1.

The scandal caused by Kidd's piratical doings under a commission from the crown, the political use made of it in Parliament, and the legend of a vast hoard of buried treasure, have conferred on him a celebrity not justified by his exploits. As he appears in the Company's records, he showed none of the picturesque daredevilry that distinguished many of the sea rovers whose names are less known. No desperate adventure or hard-fought action stand to his credit. Wherever we get a glimpse of his character it shows nothing but mean, calculating cunning; and to the end he posed as the simple, innocent man who was shamefully misjudged. His crew were always discontented and ready to desert. He had none of the lavish open-handedness that made the fraternity welcome in so many ports. Every, Teach, England, and a dozen others in his place, would have thrown the commission to the winds, and sailed the seas under the red flag.

Kidd's ruling idea appears to have been that he could hoodwink the world as to his doings under cover of his commission: so that when he heard of the charges against him he believed he could disarm his accusers by sheer impudence. At his trial he attempted to lay all the blame on his crew, and vowed he was 'the innocentest person of them all,' and all the witnesses were perjured. Whatever touch of misdirected heroism was to be found in any pirate, it was certainly not to be found in Kidd. He was altogether a contemptible rascal, and had no claims to be a popular hero.

Though Littleton's squadron captured no pirate ships, its presence till the autumn of 1700 had a salutary effect.[4] Some made their submission, and the number who continued to ply their trade was greatly reduced. Many of them were glad to leave a calling that had now become hazardous, in which they had been unwillingly forced to join, while the renewal of the war in Europe furnished a more legitimate outlet for the most turbulent spirits, in the shape of privateering.

North, after making his submission to Littleton, thought better of it, seeing the date of grace had expired, and refused to leave Madagascar. There he remained for several years, fighting and subduing the natives round St. Mary's, till he was finally killed by them. His comrades 'continued the war' for seven years till they had completely subdued the country round.

On the 18th December, 1699, the *Loyal Merchant*, Captain Lowth, East Indiaman, lying in Table Bay, saw a small vessel of sixty tons enter the harbour under English colours. This proved to be the *Margaret* of New York. Lowth's suspicions being awakened, he sent for the captain and some of the crew, who 'confessed the whole matter,' and were promptly put in irons. The *Margaret* was seized, in spite of Dutch protests. Two days later came in the *Vine*, pink, from St. Mary's, with a number of 'passengers' on board. These were pirates on their way to New England, to make their submission, among them Chivers and Culliford. Lowth would have seized them also, but the Dutch interfered, and the behaviour of the Dutch admiral became so threatening that Lowth cut short his stay and made sail for Bombay, which he reached safely, taking with him the *Margaret* and eighteen prisoners. On reaching England, Culliford was tried and condemned, but respited, as has already been mentioned.

While Kidd lay in Newgate awaiting trial, an Act was passed for the more effectual suppression of piracy. Experience had shown that it was useless to issue proclamations against individuals, but that some new machinery must be created to deal with the gigantic evil that threatened to become chronic. Under a former act, passed in the reign of Henry VIII., the Lord High Admiral, or his lieutenant, or his commissary, had been empowered to try pirates; but the procedure had long fallen into abeyance. It had been found almost impossible to bring offenders in distant seas to justice, to say nothing of the cost and trouble of bringing them to England for trial.

Now it was enacted that courts of seven persons might be formed

---

4. One small Arab vessel that rashly attacked the *Harwich*, mistaking it for a merchant vessel, was disposed of with a broadside.

for the trial of pirates at any place at sea or upon land, in any of His Majesty's islands, plantations, colonies, dominions, forts, or factories. It was necessary that at least one of the seven should be the chief of an English factory, the governor or a member of council in a plantation or colony, or the commander of a King's ship. These courts had powers of capital punishment, and also had power to treat all persons who gave assistance or countenance to pirates as accessories, and liable to the same punishments as pirates. The act was to be in force for seven years only. In 1706 it was renewed for seven years, and in 1714 again for five years.

The amnesty granted to some pirates, the hanging of others,[5] and the new Act of Parliament, caused a great abatement of the evil. The Madagascar settlements still flourished, but for a time European trade was free from attack. Littleton's squadron had gone home, and was replaced by two royal ships, the *Severn* and the *Scarborough*, which effected nothing against the pirates, but served by their presence to keep them quiet.

The *Severn* and *Scarborough* sailed from England in May, 1703, under Commodore Richards, who died at Johanna in the following March. The command was then taken by Captain Harland, who visited Madagascar and Mauritius, where two men were arrested, who afterwards made their escape at Mohilla. The two ships returned to England in October, 1705.

Hamilton tells us how a...

> Scots ship commanded by one Millar did the public more service in destroying them, than all the chargeable squadrons that have been sent in quest of them; for, with a cargo of strong ale and brandy, which he carried to sell them, in *anno* 1704, he killed above 500 of them by carousing, although they took his ship and cargo as a present from him, and his men entered, most of them into the society of the pirates.

---

5. Twenty were condemned and hung in one batch, in June, 1700; one of the *Mocha* mutineers among them. This was probably Guillam, to whom Kidd had given a passage to America from Madagascar, and was supposed to have been the man who stabbed Captain Edgecombe.

CHAPTER 3

The Rise of Conajee Angria

Europeans were not the only offenders. The Delhi emperor, who claimed universal dominion on land, made no pretension to authority at sea. So long as the Mocha fleet did not suffer, merchants were left to take care of themselves. There was no policing of the sea, and every trader had to rely on his own efforts for protection. The people of the Malabar coast were left to pursue their hereditary vocation of piracy unmolested.

The Greek author of the *Periplus of the Erythraean Sea*, who wrote in the first century of our era, mentions the pirates infesting the coast between Bombay and Goa. Two hundred years before Vasco da Gama had shown the way to India by sea, Marco Polo had told Europe of the Malabar pirates.

> And you must know that from this Kingdom of Melibar, and from, another near it called Gozurat, there go forth every year more than a hundred *corsair* vessels on cruize. These pirates take with them their wives and children, and stay out the whole summer. Their method is to join in fleets of 20 or 30 of these pirate vessels together, and then they form what they call a sea cordon, that is, they drop off till there is an interval of 5 or 6 miles between ship and ship, so that they cover something like a hundred miles of sea, and no merchant ship can escape them. For when any one *corsair* sights a vessel a signal is made by fire or smoke, and then the whole of them make for this, and seize the merchants and plunder them. After they have plundered they let them go, saying, 'Go along with you and get more gain, and that mayhap will fall to us also!' But now the merchants are aware of this, and go so well manned and armed, and with such

great ships, that they don't fear the *corsairs*. Still mishaps do befal them at times.[1]

From the Persian Gulf to Cape Comorin the whole coast was beset by native pirates, and, with the rise of the Mahratta power, the evil increased. Petty chiefs sometimes levied blackmail by giving passports to those who would pay for them, claiming the right to plunder all ships that did not carry their passes; but often the formality was dispensed with. Owing to the paucity of records of the early days, and the more serious hostility of the Portuguese and Dutch, we hear little of the losses sustained from native pirates, except when some ship with a more valuable cargo than usual was captured. Fryer tells us how, in his day, a rock off Mangalore was known as Sacrifice Island, "in remembrance of a bloody butchery on some English by the pirate Malabars." He further tells us how, in 1674, between Goa and Vingorla, he took part in an attack on a pirate ship that they came on as it was plundering a prize it had just taken, while the Dutch watched the engagement from the shore.

> We soon made him yield his prize to engage with us, which they did briskly for two hours, striving to board us, casting stink-pots among us, which broke without any execution, but so frightened our rowers, that we were forced to be severe to restrain them. They plied their chambers and small shot, and slung stones, flourishing their targets and darting long lances. They were well manned in a boat ten times as big as our barge, and at least sixty fighting men besides rowers. We had none to manage our small gun, (the gunner having deserted at Goa).

However, the pirates were beaten off, and Fryer and his companions were mightily praised by the Dutch. These pirates hailed probably from Vingorla, where the Sawunt Waree chief, known in those days as the '*Kempsant*,'[2] carried on a brisk piratical trade. The name was a corruption of Khem Sawunt, a common name of the Vingorla chiefs; the Portuguese changed it into Quemar Santo, 'the saint burner,' on account of his sacrilegious treatment of their churches.

There were no more determined pirates than the Arabs of Muscat and the Sanganians of Beyt and Dwarka, who, between them, intercepted the trade of the Persian Gulf, while the *Coolee* rovers of Guzarat took their toll of the plunder. In 1683 the Company's ship

---
1. Yule's *Marco Polo*.
2. The *Kempason* and *King Kemshew* of Downing.

President was attacked by the Muscat Arabs with two ships and four *grabs*, and fought a gallant action. The *grabs*[3] were generally two-masted ships, from one hundred and fifty to three hundred tons burden, built to draw very little water, and excellent sailers, especially in the light winds prevalent on the Western coast. They had no bowsprit, but the main-deck was continued into a long overhanging prow. The favourite mode of using them was for two or three of them to run aboard their victim at the same time, and attack, sword in hand, along the prow. Being built for fighting, and not for trade, they could sail round the clumsy merchantmen that hailed from the Thames, and, if pressed, could find safety in the shallow bays and mouths of rivers along the coast. Three *grabs* grappled the *President* at once, but the boarders were beaten back, and all three were blown up and sunk, on which the rest of the squadron made off. The *President* was set on fire in sixteen places, and lost eleven men killed and thirty-three wounded.

In the following year the *Josiah ketch* was attacked by the Sanganians while at anchor, and in the heat of the engagement blew up. A few of the crew saved themselves in a skiff, but the greater number perished, among them the commander, Lieutenant Pitts, whose father was known in Bombay as 'the drunken lieutenant.'

In September, 1685, the *Phoenix*, a British man-of-war that had been sent for a two-years' cruise in Indian waters, was attacked by a Sanganian vessel that mistook her for a merchantman. It was almost a calm, and Captain Tyrrell hoisted out his boats to capture the Sanganian ship, but they were beaten off, so he sunk her with a couple of broadsides. Forty-one of the pirates were picked up, but many of them refused quarter, and one hundred and seven were killed or drowned. The *Phoenix* had three men killed, one wounded, and two drowned. According to Hamilton, Sir George Byng, the first lieutenant, was dangerously wounded; but the log of the *Phoenix* is silent on that point, though it gives the names of the casualties.

Three years later, the *Thomas*, Captain Lavender, was less fortunate. Attacked by four Beyt ships, after a brave resistance, the *Thomas* took fire, and all on board perished.

Their depredations were not confined to the sea. In 1697 some Beyt pirates landed and plundered a village within sight of Broach.

But the losses occasioned by native pirates were at first nearly lost sight of in the more serious losses occasioned by European *corsairs*.

---

3. From the Arabic *ghorab*, 'a raven.'

As for those Sanganians and those Mallabars and professed pirates, (wrote the directors in 1699), we see no cause why you should not wage an offensive as well as a defensive war against them when they fall in your way: but it is hardly worth the while to keep small vessels to look after them, for they are poor rogues and nothing to be got of them to answer any charge.

In 1707, the year of Aurungzeeb's death, the pirates of the Persian Gulf made a great haul of plunder. A squadron of them made their way to the Red Sea, waylaid the Mocha fleet, and returned home laden with booty. In the following year, a squadron of fourteen Arab ships from the Gulf, carrying from thirty to fifty guns, and with seven thousand men on board, appeared on the Malabar coast and surprised Honore, Mangalore, and Balasore(?); but the people, having lately been plundered by the *Seedee*, were ready with their arms, and beat them off with the loss of four or five hundred men.

The Arab insolencies are often in the thoughts of the court, (wrote the London directors), but the court fears they shall not be able to do anything effectually to check their growing strength during the present war, which finds employment for all our naval force. Further, the court sympathizes with Madras on their severe losses by the pirates, which puts a damp on the Company's trade, and affects their revenues.

Annoying as were the losses that were suffered from the chronic depredations of the Arabs and Sanganians, they sank into insignificance when compared with the troubles experienced on the rise to power of Conajee (Kanhojee) Angria. The growth of the Mahratta power under Sivajee had been accompanied by the formation of a formidable fleet which harried the coast of the Concan, and against which the *Seedee* chief, the emperor's representative afloat, could hardly maintain himself. In 1698 Conajee Angria succeeded to the command of the Mahratta navy, with the title of Darya-Sáranga. In the name of the Satara chief he was master of the whole coast from Bombay to Vingorla, with the exception of the Seedee's territory.

Defenceless towns as far south as Travancore were attacked and plundered, while, at sea, vessels of native merchants were preyed upon. For a time he seems not to have meddled with the Company's vessels; as the size of his ships increased, he grew bolder, and, in 1702, his doings began to excite apprehension. In that year he was addressed to release a small trading vessel from Calicut with six Englishmen on board that had been seized and carried into one of his harbours. What had roused his anger against the English does not appear, but a month later we find him sending word to Bombay that he would give the English cause to remember the name of Conajee Angria, a threat that he carried out only too well.

Two years later we find him described as a 'Rebel Independent of the Rajah Sivajee,' and Mr. Reynolds was deputed to find him and tell him that he could not be permitted searching, molesting, or seizing vessels in Bombay waters: to which he returned a defiant answer, that he had done many benefits to the English, who had broken faith with him, and henceforth he would seize their vessels wherever he could find them. In 1707 his ships attacked the *Bombay* frigate, which was blown up after a brief engagement, and for the next half-century Angrian piracy was a scourge to the European trade of the West coast. In 1710 Conajee Angria seized and fortified Kennery, and his ships fought the *Godolphin* for two days, within sight of Bombay, but were finally beaten off. He had now grown so powerful that, in 1711, the Directors were told he could take any ship except the largest Europe ones; "along the coast from Surat to Dabul he takes all private merchant vessels he meets."

Owing to the minority and imprisonment of Sivajee's grandson, Sahoojee,[4] the Mahrattas were torn by internal divisions, in which Conajee Angria played his part. On the death of Aurungzeeb, Sahoojee regained his liberty, and was seated on the *guddee* of Satara. Owing to his want of hardihood, and weakness of character, the dissensions continued, and Sivajee's kingdom seemed to be on the point of breaking up into a number of independent chiefships. Among those aiming at independence was Conajee Angria. In 1713, an army sent against him under the Peishwa, Bhyroo Punt, was defeated, and Bhyroo Punt taken prisoner. It was reported that Conajee was preparing to march on Satara. Ballajee Rao, who afterwards became Peishwa, was placed at the head of such troops as could hastily be collected together, and opened negotiations with Conajee.

An accommodation was arrived at, by which Conajee agreed to acknowledge allegiance to Satara, in return for which he was confirmed in command of the fleet, with the title of Surkheil, and granted twenty-six forts and fortified places with their dependent villages.[5]

---

4. Known in the English annals of the time as the Sow Rajah, and the South Rajah.
5. The principal forts were Kennery, Colaba, Severndroog, Viziadroog or Gheriah, Jyeghur, Deoghur, Manikdroog, Futtehghur, Oochitghur; and Yeswuntdroog.

The first result of this treaty was a war with the *Seedee*, who had enjoyed some of the places in question for a number of years. Conajee was supported by the Satara arms, and the *Seedee* was forced to submit to the loss.

To all intents and purposes, Conajee was now an independent chief. He was the recognized master of a strip of territory between the sea and the western *ghauts*, extending from Bombay harbour to Vingorla, excluding the *Seedee's* territories, a tract, roughly speaking, about two hundred and forty miles in length by forty miles in breadth. With his harbours strongly fortified, while the western *ghauts* made his territories difficult of access by land, he was in a position to bid defiance to all enemies. Moreover, he was the recognized chief of the hardy coast population of hereditary seamen, who to this day furnish the best lascars to our Indian marine.

Angria's exploits on land had not interfered with his interests at sea. In November, 1712, he captured the governor of Bombay's armed yacht, together with the *Anne ketch* from Carwar.[6] In the engagement, Mr. Chown, chief of the Carwar factory, was killed, and his young wife, a widow for the second time at the age of eighteen, became Angria's prisoner. A month later, the *Somers* and *Grantham*, East Indiamen, on their voyage from England to Bombay, were attacked by a grab and a gallivat belonging to Angria, off the coast north of Goa. Owing to there being a calm at the time, the East Indiamen were unable to bring their guns to bear: "for which reason and by ye earnest intercession of ye whole ship's company to ye captain" the boats of the *Somers* and *Grantham* were hoisted out, and an attempt was made to board the pirates. The attack was beaten off with the loss of four men killed and seventeen wounded; but the pirates found the entertainment so little to their liking that they made off.

On hearing of the capture of the governor's yacht, the Portuguese wrote to propose a joint attack on Angria. A few months before, he had captured the greater part of a Portuguese '*armado*,' and disabled a thirty-gun man-of-war that was convoying it. Governor Aislabie declined the Portuguese offer, but it had the effect of bringing Angria to terms. Thinking it politic to make peace with the English, while his affairs with the *rajah* of Satara were still unsettled, he sent a messenger to Bombay, offering to deliver up all vessels, goods, and captives taken from the Company, if an Englishman of credit was sent to him to settle on terms of peace for the future.

---

6. See *An Englishwoman in India* following.

Aislabie demanded that in future English ships should be free from molestation; that no ships of any nation coming into Bombay should be interfered with between Mahim and Kennery; that English merchants should have liberty of trade in Angria's ports, on payment of the usual dues; and that Angria should be responsible for any damage done in future by the ships belonging to his Mahratta superiors. In return, the governor engaged to give passes only to ships belonging to merchants recognized by the Company, and to allow Angria's people full trading facilities in Bombay, on the usual dues being paid. To these terms Angria agreed, but failed to get the governor's consent to additional terms of an egregious nature; that he should be supplied by the Company with powder and shot on payment; that a place should be assigned to him to make powder in; that if pressed by his enemies, he should be assisted by the Company; that merchant ships should not be convoyed in or out of Bombay harbour.

There remained the duty of sending him 'an Englishman of credit' to 'deliver him the articles.' The council, 'knowing him to be a man of ill principles,' thought it improper to order any man on such a risky service, but Lieutenant Mackintosh, in consideration of a gratuity of one thousand *rupees*, undertook to go, and departed for Colaba, with *Rs.*30,000 as ransom for the European prisoners, the convention sealed with the council's seal, and ships to bring back the restored goods.

And so for a time there was security from Angria's attacks, but, with his hands free on the Satara side, and in a more secure position than ever, it was not likely that the peace would be of long continuance. With a fleet of armed vessels carrying thirty and forty guns apiece, with Kennery island in his possession within sight of Bombay harbour, Angria and his successors continued to be a menace to the existence of Bombay, while the Angrian territory became the Alsatia of the Indian seas, where desperadoes of all nationalities were made welcome.

The next few years saw an enormous increase of piracy in the Indian seas. Angria was practically secure in his fastnesses along the coast, and plundered every ship not strong enough to defend itself. His finest vessels were commanded by Europeans, generally Dutch. The signing of the Peace of Utrecht brought a fresh swarm of European adventurers to reap the harvest of the seas. The privateersmen, disregarding the peace, under pretence of making war on France and Spain, plundered ships of all nations. Conden,[7] White, England, Taylor, and many others,

---

7. The name of this pirate is also given as Congdon and Condent.

made Madagascar their headquarters, and emulated the feats of Every and Kidd. The Beyt pirates were as mischievous as ever, while the Muscat Arabs could muster, in 1715, a ship of seventy-four guns, two of sixty, one of fifty, eighteen carrying thirty-two to twelve guns each, and a host of smaller vessels carrying never less than four guns. The Company was forced to rely on its own exertions, as there was not a single King's ship in Indian waters. The few armed vessels belonging to Bombay convoyed the more valuable vessels along the coast. The larger ships, that made the ocean voyage between India and Europe, sailed in company for mutual protection.

Chapter 4

An Active Governor

On the 26th December, 1715, Bombay was *en fête*. The East Indiamen *Stanhope* and *Queen* had arrived from England, bringing the new governor, Mr. Charles Boone, and three new councillors. His predecessor, Mr. Aislabie, had sailed for England in October. At the landing-place the newcomers were met by the late council and the principal inhabitants and merchants of Bombay. Thirty-one pieces of ordnance greeted them with a salvo, and, as they put foot on shore, three companies of soldiers saluted them with three volleys of small arms.

Boone was a man of very different stamp from his predecessors. The quarrels, intrigues, and self-seeking that had been so disastrous a feature during the tenure of office of Child, Waite, and Gayer were abhorrent to him. He was a zealous servant of the Company, whose interests he did his best to promote with the inadequate means at his disposal. In coming up the coast he had touched at the places where the Company had factories, and by the time of his arrival in Bombay he had fully realized that the pirate question demanded serious treatment.

Bombay was then an open town, only the factory being fortified. Soon after receiving Bombay from the crown, the directors had ordered it to be fortified, but had refused to employ skilled officers, because "we know that it is natural to engineers to contrive curiosities that are very expensive." The only protection to the town was such as was afforded by a number of Martello towers along the shore. Nineteen years before Boone's time the Muscat Arabs had made a descent on Salsette, ravaging, burning, and plundering as they pleased, killing the Portuguese priests and carrying off fourteen hundred captives into slavery. Since then the formidable power of Angria had arisen, but nothing had been done to improve the defences of the settlement. Boone's first care was to trace out an enclosing wall, the building of which was to be paid for by contributions from the native merchants.

At the same time he set to work to build fighting ships. Within a few months of his arrival, the *Britannia*, eighteen guns, built at Carwar, the *Fame*, sixteen guns, built at Surat, and the *Revenge*, sixteen guns, built at Bombay, were flying the Company's flag. It was easier to build ships than to get sailors to man them, in view of the miserable pay given by the Company, and the attractions of service under native chiefs. Many of the crews were foreigners, who were ready enough to take service with Angria, if the inclination took them, and the bulk of the crews were Indian lascars.

A few months later, the *Victory*, twenty-four guns, was launched, and two years after his arrival, Boone had at his disposal a fine fleet consisting of nineteen frigates, *grabs, ketches, gallivats*, and rowing galleys, carrying two hundred and twenty guns, besides a bomb vessel and a fireship. With such a force much ought to have been accomplished, but throughout his tenure of office Boone's efforts were crippled by the incompetency and indiscipline of those on whom he depended to carry out his designs: while the efficiency of the ships was diminished by their employment to carry cargoes along the coast.

In March, 1717, Bombay was stirred by the arrival of a private ship, the *Morning Star*, which had escaped the Beyt pirates after a long and severe encounter. The affair is described by Hamilton; but he modestly conceals the fact that he was himself in command of the *Morning Star*, of which he was chief owner. The ship was on its way from Gombroon to Surat, with a valuable cargo, of which the pirates had intelligence; and two squadrons were fitted out to waylay her. On the 20th March she was assailed by eight pirate ships, the largest of which was of five hundred tons, three others being of nearly three hundred tons each, and the rest galleys and *shybars*, or half-galleys. Between them they carried about two thousand men.

On board the *Morning Star* there were only six Europeans, a number of native merchants, and about thirty-five or forty lascars, about half of whom were trustworthy. The first attack was made by the largest of the pirate ships alone, and was beaten off with loss to the assailants. In the fight, Hamilton had his thigh pierced through with a lance. For the rest of that day and the whole of the following no further attack was made; but the pirates hung around planning another assault. On the 22nd it was delivered. The two largest pirates ran the *Morning Star* aboard, one on her bow and one on her quarter, while three others poured their crews across the decks of their comrades.

For four hours a desperate combat ensued, the six vessels being locked together. In the heat of the fight the native merchants went on board the pirates to try and ransom themselves, and were accompanied by half the lascars who deserted their commander; only the Europeans and seventeen lascars remained to fight the ship. She caught fire in three places, the poop and half-deck being burned through. The two pirate ships likewise caught fire, which caused them to slacken their efforts. In the confusion Hamilton managed to disengage his ship, and made sail; the five pirate ships being so entangled together that they were unable to pursue, and two of them so injured as to be in a sinking condition.

So Hamilton brought off his ship in safety, after as gallant a feat of arms as was ever performed. Seven of his men were killed, and about the same number wounded, and finding no surgeon in Surat, he came on to Bombay. The native merchants who were carried off by the pirates were made to pay a ransom of £6000, and brought back word that great slaughter had been done on the pirates, while their commodore lost his head, on returning to Beyt, for allowing so rich a prize to escape.

In April, Boone sent down the *Fame* and the *Britannia*, under Commodore Weekes, to attack Vingorla. They carried a company of *sepoys* under Stanton, one of the Company's military officers. On the way they were joined by the *Revenge*, and they also had with them ten or twelve *gallivats*. Weekes appears to have been timid and incompetent, while the force was altogether insufficient for the purpose. Several days were spent in trying to find a landing-place, without success, on the rocky, surf-beaten shore, while the fortress was bombarded from different points. A violent quarrel occurred between Weekes and Stanton, and the expedition returned to Bombay.

This was the first, but not the most serious, of Boone's failures. It was characteristic of all the warlike expeditions he sent out, that while he was indefatigable in preparing armaments, all other details requisite to success were left to chance. The council resolved that Weekes was unfit to be commodore, and deposed him. To fill his place the veteran Alexander Hamilton, whose recent defence of the *Morning Star* had shown his fighting capacity, was induced to relinquish his private trade, and made commander-in-chief of all the Company's frigates on a salary of *Rs.*80 a month. His ship, the *Morning Star,* was also hired by the council.

As soon as the monsoon was over, he was required to conduct an expedition to relieve the Carwar factory, which was beleaguered by the Sunda Rajah. The chief of the factory at this time was Mr. George Taylor. In the spring of 1717, a Bombay merchant's ship carrying an English pass and flying English colours had been seized by the *rajah*, who imprisoned the crew. Demands for their surrender were being made, when, in May, the *Elizabeth*, belonging to Mr. Strutt, a private merchant at Surat, with £15,000 worth of treasure on board, went ashore near Carwar. Before more than half the treasure could be removed in safety to the factory, the *rajah* sent down an armed force to seize the ship as jetsam, imprisoned the captain and crew, and laid siege to the factory.

So Hamilton was sent down with a small squadron and some troops. Fortunately the factory was exceptionally well provisioned. On the 30th August, the *Morning Star*, with five *gallivats* and a sloop, arrived off Carwar, and blockaded the harbour till the arrival of Hamilton and the rest of the force on the 12th September. In command of the land force was Midford, one of the Company's factors. On the 13th, the troops were landed, under Midford and Stanton, in a heavy surf which drove the *gallivats*[1] on shore and upset them, throwing the whole party into the water. Midford, with some of his men, struggled on shore, but Stanton was taken out of the water senseless.[2]

In the midst of this scene of confusion they were suddenly charged by the *rajah's* horsemen. Half drowned, undisciplined, and with their ammunition spoiled by water, they could make only a feeble resistance. Midford and his English serjeant, Hill, were desperately wounded and made prisoners, together with five Europeans and forty-seven *topasses*, while sixty men were killed and two *gallivats* lost. The wretched *topasses* had their noses cut off, five European heads were stuck up in derision before the factory, while Midford and Hill were alternately cajoled and threatened to induce them to take service with the *rajah*.

In consequence of this disaster, the factory sued for peace, but the *rajah's* terms were so humiliating that they were rejected, and it was decided to await further reinforcements from Bombay; but two

---

1. *Galleywats*, or *gallivats*, were large rowing-boats with two masts, of forty to seventy tons, and carrying four to eight guns.
2. In a letter, three years later, on the conduct of military officers, it is stated that "Stanton was drunk the time he should have gone upon action at Carwar."

months elapsed before their arrival. Meanwhile, a post of four hundred men was established on shore to guard the water-supply required for daily use. This gave rise to a skirmish, which put some heart into the invaders. Early one morning the post was attacked by the enemy, who found, to their surprise, that they had come under fire of the guns of some small vessels Hamilton had anchored close inshore. After an hour's cannonade, they broke and fled, pursued by the party on shore, who accounted for some two hundred of them.

Encouraged by this success, Stanton continued to harass the *rajah* by small night attacks, and by burning some of his villages, while at sea they did him more damage by intercepting his ships laden with salt and other necessaries, and especially three, bringing Arab horses from Muscat; though the captors were much troubled in providing water and provender for them. Meanwhile, the factory, which was five or six miles up the river, on the north bank, continued to be invested, and in order to prevent any communication with the squadron, a boom was laid across the river, commanded by a battery on the south side. In spite of this, communication was kept up through the Portuguese factory, and, more than once, Lieutenant Forbes contrived to pass in and out in a rowing-boat, but it was impossible to send in provisions.

About this time we find Hamilton reporting to Bombay—

The recruits from Goa had a skirmish at break of day, on 28th September, with the enemy, wherein they behaved themselves bravely, but that on an attempt to burn some villages afterwards, they advised the enemy of it, and deserted with some arms and *granadoes*.

At last the looked-for reinforcements arrived from Bombay, under Captain Gordon, raising the whole strength of the expedition to 2250 men, including seamen, and a landing in force was determined on. Two of the prizes had been equipped as floating batteries, with shot-proof bulwarks, and were laid ashore to engage the Rajah's batteries. At four o'clock in the morning of the 16th November, 1250 men were put ashore, under Gordon, without hindrance from the enemy, who were ready to take to flight before such a force. Gordon's idea was to advance in a hollow square, which, in spite of Hamilton's sneer at him as a 'freshwater land officer,' was a good enough formation in the circumstances; but so much time was consumed in getting the men into the required formation, owing to the inexperience and want of discipline among both officers and men, that the enemy took heart again and advanced to meet them.

When the square at last moved forward, with Gordon at their head, they were met with a hot fire, and Gordon was a mark for every aim. Before long he fell, shot in the breast, and Captain Smith, 'commonly called Old Woman,' on whom the command devolved, at once gave the word to retreat. According to Hamilton, 'he pulled off his red coat and vanished.' The *rajah's* horsemen charged down, sword in hand, on the disordered ranks; the men threw down their arms and fled to the boats, leaving some two hundred and fifty of their number dead on the field. Fortunately, the floating batteries covered the embarkation, and prevented the enemy, who had suffered some loss, from gathering the spoils of the fallen. Eighty seamen were sent on shore, and brought back about two hundred muskets that had been thrown away in flight, most of them loaded. Thus ingloriously ended the attempts at landing.

The factory was by this time reduced to great straits for food, and this fresh disaster made peace imperative; the *rajah*, in spite of his success so far, was anxious to come to an accommodation. The expense of maintaining so many armed men threatened to ruin him; the sea blockade and the detention of the horses were events on which he had not reckoned: and, worse still, his northern borders were harried by the Sow Rajah, 'which made him incline very much towards a peace:' so an agreement was quickly arrived at, and, on the 29th November, peace was proclaimed on easy terms for both parties. The expedition had cost the Company *Rs.*68,372 in hard cash. The inability of the landing force to advance beyond range of the ships' guns bears witness to their military incapacity.

His short experience of six months under the Company had completely disgusted Alexander Hamilton. Immediately on his return to Bombay he resigned his post as commander-in-chief of their ships-of-war, and resumed business as a private trader. His relations with the military officers during the expedition appear to have been satisfactory, but against Taylor, the head of the Carwar factory, he formulated a series of charges, accusing him of having been the cause of the trouble with the *rajah*, through his indiscretion and bad faith. Taylor retaliated by accusing Hamilton of not having taken proper measures to relieve the factory. The council investigated the charges, and contented themselves with cautioning Taylor to behave better in future.

The unfortunate *topasses*, who had had their noses cut off, were formed into a company of marines, and had their pay augmented to

Rs.5 a month.[3] In this odd way the Bombay Marine Battalion appears to have had its origin.

We get some idea of the Sunda *rajahs* of the period in a letter from Carwar, dated the 20th January, 1698.

> He (the Sunda Rajah) is so excessive craving after money, that he is about sacrificing twelve men and twelve women with child, to get two pots of treasure which one of his magicians tells him lies buried near his palace.

While these events were taking place at Carwar, Boone found himself involved in trouble with Angria. For some time after the treaty made by Aislabie, Angria had respected Bombay trading ships, but of late he had begun to show his teeth again. In the beginning of 1716 he had made prize of a Company's boat in sight of the harbour, and of another belonging to a private merchant. Four private ships from Mahim, valued at 30,000 *xeraphims*, were also captured by him, and his ships trading to Bombay refused to pay harbour dues. While Hamilton was engaged at Carwar, Angria's fleet attacked and took the *Success*, East Indiaman, on its way from Surat. With an impoverished exchequer, a force weakened and disorganized by the Carwar adventure, and no ammunition in his magazine, Boone found himself in no condition to take active measures for the present.

In the vain hope of bringing Angria to reason, a letter of expostulation was written, which met with a hostile response, quickly followed by the capture of the *Otter*, a Bengal ship. A second letter of defiance was received, so, on the 7th May, in spite of inadequate resources, the Council resolved on striking a blow. An expedition against Gheriah was determined on, and twenty *gallivats* were sent down, manned with *sepoys*, to retake, if possible, the captured vessels, "if they were attacked, to repel force by force, and if possible plunder his country." The official record of the expedition is as follows:—

> *4th June.*—Two *gallivats* returned having plundered a town in Angria's country, and brought away sixteen prisoners.
>
> *9th June.*—Returned our *gallivats*, having by mismanagement of the chief officer lost about fifty men and destroyed one town of Angria's.

Downing, who was present, gives an account of the attack on Gheriah, though he makes a mistake as to the date. As it is the only ac-

---

3. Bombay Consultations, 22nd January, 1718.

count we have of what took place, it will be better to give it in his own words.

On the 10th of the same instant the President reviewed the land forces on shore, and saw all things put in good and sufficient order. Major Vane, chief engineer for the Company, had tried all the mortars and coehorns, then fitted and stocked for the expedition. Mr. John Minims was appointed chief engineer for the direction of these mortars and coehorns, which did great service. We proceeded down the coast for Gerey, which is not above twelve hours' sail from Bombay, where we with all our navy soon arrived, and run boldly into the harbour. Captain Berlew (Bellew?) Commodore, and ranged a line from the eastermost part of the fortifications to the outer part of the harbour.

Keeping all our small galleys and galleywats on the off-side under shelter. But they had strong fortifications on both sides; so that we left our strongest ships in the harbour, to make a breach in the walls, in order to storm the castle. The rocks were very high, and so slippery that one could hardly stand without a staff, and consequently not a place convenient to draw men up in any posture of defence.

We endeavoured to get the fireship in, but could not; for on the east part of the fort they had a cove or creek, where they had laid up a great part of their fleet, and had got a strong boom across the same; so that we could not annoy them any otherwise than by throwing our bombs and coehorns very thick into the garrison, which we did for a considerable time, and were in hopes after the first and second day's siege, that we should have drove them out of that strong castle, but we soon found that the place was impregnable.

For as we kept throwing our shells as fast as we could in regular time, cooling our chambers before we loaded again; after we had beat over two or three houses in the castle, the shells fell on the rocks in the inside the castle, and their weight and force of falling would break them without so much as their blowing up.....As to storming the walls, they were so high that our scaling ladders would not near reach the top of them ....

After the second day we landed all our forces, taking the opportunity of the tide....We got them all on shore, and marched up the country, without molestation; only now and then the castle would let fly a shot or two, which did us small damage. We attempted to march the army down to their shipping, and to set them on fire; but when we came within a mile of the place the land was all swampy, and so very muddy by the spring tides flowing over that we could not proceed.

On our retreat they galled us very much by firing from the castle, we being obliged to come near the castle walls to take our forces off again. Here the gallant Captain Gordon was slightly wounded again. . . . . I question whether there were a hundred men in the castle during the time of the siege. . . .

We drew off our forces on the 18th April, and went up to Bombay to repair our frigates and take care of our wounded men, of whom we had a considerable number.

In no way discouraged by the failure, Boone at once set to work to prepare for a fresh attack on Angria. This time it was determined that Kennery, within sight of Bombay harbour, should be the object of attack, and all through the monsoon preparations were made.

CHAPTER 5

The Company's Servants

It may be useful here to consider the difference in the men sent out, by England, to the East and West Indies during the seventeenth and part of the eighteenth centuries. To the West Indies went out representatives of the landed gentry from every county in England. Charters were obtained from the crown, conferring estates, and sometimes whole islands, on men of ancient families. Slaves were cheap, and sugar cultivation brought in great wealth; the whole machinery of English life was reproduced in the tropics—counties, parishes; sheriffs, rectories, tithes, an established church, etc. The same causes that sent the cavaliers to Virginia, sent a smaller migration to the West Indies.

At the Restoration, the men who had conquered Jamaica for Cromwell were unwilling to return to England. Monmouth's rebellion and the expulsion of the Stuarts produced a fresh influx. But, whether Cavaliers or Roundheads or Jacobites, they came from the landholding class in England. The evidence may still be read in old West Indian graveyards, where the crumbling monuments show the carefully engraved armorial bearings, and the inscriptions record the families and homes in England from which those whom they commemorate had sprung.

In the East Indies nothing of the kind was possible. The acquisition of land for agriculture was out of the question. Trade was the only opening, and that was monopolized by the Company. Except as a servant of the Company, an Englishman had no legal status in the East. The chief profits went to the shareholders in London. If at the end of twenty-five years or so a Company's servant could return to England with a few thousands made by private trade, he was a fortunate man. Private traders and a few of the governors were alone able to make fortunes. The shaking of the *pagoda* tree did not begin till after Plassey. The result was that the men who went to India were of a totally different class from those who went to America and the West Indies; they were young men from small trading families in London, Greenwich, and Deptford, or from seaport towns like Bristol and Plymouth. Among them were some restless and adventurous spirits who found life in England too tame or too burdensome. For such men India was long regarded as a useful outlet.

"If you cannot devise expedients to send contributions, or procure credit, all is lost, and I must go to the Indies," wrote William the Third, in bitter humour, at a desperate crisis in his affairs. Fryer tells us (1698) how the Company had entertained Bluecoat boys as apprentices for seven years, after which time they were to be made writers, if able to furnish the required security. The salaries they received from the Company were only nominal. A Bombay pay-list of January, 1716, shows us the official salaries at that time. The governor received £300 *per annum*. Next to him came eight merchants, who with him constituted the council, and received respectively, one £100, one £70, two £50, and four £40 each. Below them came three senior factors at £30 each, three junior factors at £15, and seven writers at £5.[1]

The tale is completed by the accountant and the chaplain, who received £100 each. A writer on entering the service had to find security for £500, which was increased to £1000 when he rose to be a factor. The unmarried servants of the Company were lodged at the Company's expense; the married ones received a lodging allowance, and a public table was maintained. In fact, the Company treated them as if they were apprentices in a warehouse in St. Paul's Churchyard, and, when the conditions of their service are taken into account, it is not surprising that there was a considerable amount of dishonesty among them. These conditions apart, they were neither worse nor better than the men of their time.

As the original Company gained stability by the incorporation of its upstart rival established in 1698,[2] which put an end to a condition of affairs that promised to be ruinous to both, and by the grant of perpetuity issued in the year following incorporation, there was a gradual improvement in the quality of their civil servants. Though no increase

---

1. According to the Company's instructions in 1675, writers were to receive no salary at all for the first five years, and after that £10 a year. In 1699 the Court of Directors settled the salaries of merchants at £60, factors at £40, and writers at £20 *per annum* (Bruce); but in 1716 the salaries were as above stated.

2. The London Company and the English East India Company were amalgamated in 1708.

in the salaries of junior officers took place for many years afterwards, the greater facilities opened to them, for trade, attracted better men into the service, among them some cadets of good family.

Miserable as was the display of military incompetency at Carwar and on subsequent occasions, it is hardly surprising when the condition of the Company's soldiers is considered. The Company's policy was to keep officers and men in a state of degrading subjection; to prevent the officers from having any authority over their men, while pledges as to pay were often broken.

When the Company first received Bombay from the crown, the royal troops in the island were invited to remain in the Company's service on the same rank and pay, on the condition that they might resign when they pleased—a condition that made discipline impossible. The greater number of them accepted the terms. Two years later, a company was sent out under Captain Shaxton to fill vacancies. Shaxton was evidently a man of good abilities and position; one who had been trained in the stern military school of the civil wars. He was to be a factor in addition to his military command, and if, after trial, his qualifications would admit of it, he was to hold the office of deputy governor. The men were engaged for three years.

By the time he had been two years in Bombay, Shaxton found that, under the penurious rule of the Company, efficiency was impossible, while the two European companies maintained for the defence of the island could only be kept up to strength by filling the vacancies with natives. Four years later,[3] a mutiny broke out, in which Shaxton supported the demands of his men. They complained that a month's pay, promised to them on engagement, was due to them, and claimed their discharge, as their time of service had expired. President Aungier behaved with prudence and firmness. He pacified the men by granting their demands, and brought the ringleaders to trial by court-martial. Three of them were condemned to death, of whom one, Corporal Fake, was shot, and the other two pardoned. Shaxton was then brought to trial, found guilty of some of the charges, and sent to England for punishment according to the king's pleasure.

Two years later a troop of horse was formed, and sent out under Captain Richard Keigwin, who was to command the garrison on a salary of £120 a year. Keigwin was a man of good Cornish family, who had entered the King's Navy in 1665, and taken part in Monk's memorable four days' battle against the Dutch in the following year.

---

3. 1674.

When St. Helena was recaptured from the Dutch (1673), he had distinguished himself in command of the boats that made the attack, and was left as governor of the island till it was taken over by the East India Company. As a reward for his services, the Company made him their military commandant at Bombay.

Two years later again, the Company, in a fit of economy, reduced their military establishment to two lieutenants, two ensigns, and one hundred and eighty-eight rank and file. The troop of horse was disbanded, Keigwin was discharged from the service, and thirty soldiers, who had been detached to Surat to defend the factory against Sivajee, were refused any extra allowance, which caused much discontent. Before long the directors became alarmed at the defenceless state of Bombay, and sent out Keigwin again with troops and artillery, to have the chief military command and the third seat in council. To meet the expense, the other officers were made to suffer in rank and pay, and the whole of the small force fell into a dangerous state of discontent.

Among other reductions in the pay of their military force, the directors reduced the rate of exchange, a measure that affected the men as well as the officers; and, not content with making these changes prospective, insisted that the officers should refund the surplus of what they had received. Keigwin also had his personal grievance. He claimed subsistence money, like the rest of the merchants and factors, the Company's table having been abolished.[4]

After much altercation, a grant was made to him, on the condition that it would have to be refunded if disallowed by the directors. He was sick of the Company, with their greed and their selfish economies at the expense of their servants, their broken pledges and stupid changes of policy in military affairs, the intrigues of Sir John Child at Surat, and the schemes of his brother, Sir Josiah Child, in England. Like many other Englishmen, he considered the Company was an anomaly, dangerous to the authority of the crown, and his distrust was increased by the mismanagement and corruption that existed among their servants in the East.

On the 27th December, 1683, he seized Mr. Ward, the deputy governor, and such of the council as sided with him, assembled the troops, and issued a proclamation declaring the Company's authority at an end, and that the island was henceforth under the king's protection. By general consent he was elected governor, and at once proceeded to restore order. The troops and inhabitants were called on to take an

---

4. It was afterwards re-established, and again abolished in Boone's time.

oath of allegiance to the king, and to renounce their obedience to the Company, a demand that was universally complied with. Officials were appointed, grievances were redressed, and trade was encouraged, to be carried on without molestation so long as Keigwin's authority was not challenged. Money arriving from England was lodged in the fort, with a declaration that it would be employed only in defence of the island, and letters were addressed by Keigwin to the king and the Duke of York, stating his determination to hold the island for the king till His Majesty's pleasure should be known, together with the causes that had led to the revolt; one of them being the necessity of preserving it from becoming a conquest to the native powers.

Never had Bombay been so well governed as it was during the eleven months of Keigwin's rule. The *Seedee* sent a friendly deputation to him. From the *rajah* of Satara he obtained confirmation of the articles agreed on by Sivajee, a grant for the establishment of factories at Cuddalore and Thevenapatam, an exemption from duties in the Carnatic, and the payment of twelve thousand pagodas in compensation for losses sustained at different places formerly plundered by the Mahrattas. There was no disorder or bloodshed; the only thing of the kind that has been recorded being a wound received by Keigwin himself in a quarrel at table.

So great was the enthusiasm for Keigwin, that when, first commissioners, and then Sir John Child himself, came from Surat to try and re-establish the Company's authority, it was with difficulty that the crews of their vessels could be prevented from joining Keigwin and his adherents.[5] It was well for the Company that he was a man of solid character and not an adventurer. On the arrival of Sir Thomas Grantham from England in November, 1684, Keigwin surrendered the island to him, as a King's officer, on condition of a free pardon for himself and his associates, and proceeded to England.[6] The Company's treasure was intact, and, except for the dangerous spirit against the Company that had been aroused, Bombay was in a better state than it had been at the time of the revolt.

After this the Company decided to have nothing more to do with professional soldiers. It was the time when the great feeling of hostility

---

5. Bombay was subordinate to the Surat factory till 1685.
6. Four years after returning to England, Keigwin was given the command of a frigate. In 1690 he accompanied the expedition against the French in the West Indies, and fell at the head of his men in the assault of Basseterre, St. Christopher's.—*Dic. Nat. Bio.*

to a standing army was growing up in England, under the mischievous preaching of agitators, which reached its height thirteen years later. They took into their service men of low origin, devoid of military training, who would have no influence over their men, and who would submit to any treatment. Boone, writing to the directors in 1720, says—

> It is well known the Company's servants, in all the settlements I have been in, seldom keep company with the military, especially the council. Now and then they may invite one to take a dinner, which is a favour; but the men which he distinguishes are not company for your second.

The social status of the Company's officers appears later, when an Act was passed to extend the Mutiny Act to the East Indies and St. Helena, in consequence of the Company's right to exercise martial law having been questioned. In opposing the bill, the Earl of Egmont said—

> If I am rightly informed, there are some of the Company's officers of a very low character. One of them was formerly a trumpeter at a raree show in this country, and when he was discharged that honourable service he listed himself in the Company's service as a common soldier, and I suppose was made an officer by one of those governors for trumpeting to him better than any other man could do it in the country. Another, I am told, was a low sort of barber—one of our shave-for-a-penny barbers—here in London. And another of them was a butcher here, and when he is not upon duty I am told he still exercises his trade there. Can we think that such officers will not be despised by gentlemen who have the honour to bear His Majesty's commission?

He based his opposition to the bill on the unfitness of the Company's officers to exercise authority, and to the bad relations sure to arise between them and the King's officers.[7]

In quarters they were not allowed to give any orders to their men, or to have any control over them, the most trivial matters being kept in the hands of the merchants and factors. To such an extent was this carried, that for fifty years afterwards no military officer was allowed to give out the parole and countersign.[8] Their only duties were to

---

7. Hansard, 1754.
8. The first general order issued by the commander-in-chief in Madras was dated the 22nd November, 1772.

command the men when under arms. Commissions were granted and taken away by the council without reference to the directors.

Under such treatment there could be neither self-respect nor pride in their profession. Of their general behaviour, we may gather some idea from an entry concerning Lieutenant Parker at this time. He was arraigned before the council for drinking, brawling with his men, and frequenting base houses, for which the council deprived him of his commission; but as he was 'an extraordinary person in disciplining (drilling) soldiers,' he was appointed adjutant of the regiment till he should give a specimen of improved behaviour. When there was fighting to be done, the command was taken by factors and writers, who were given temporary commissions as captains, colonels, etc.

Midford, Brown, Cowan, and others we hear of in command of troops, were only soldiers for the occasion. So far back as 1676 the directors had enjoined on their civil servants to acquire a knowledge of military discipline, that in the event of any sudden attack they might bear arms. Clive was far from being the first of the Company's servants to lay down the pen for the sword, but he was the first to do so permanently.

The inferior quality of the Company's officers through the first half of the century is reflected in the fact that among the many who distinguished themselves in the hard fighting that went on from 1751 to 1764, we find only two who had not graduated in the King's service. These were Clive, who entered the Company's service as a writer, and Preston, who was sent to India as a civil engineer. Of the Company's purely military officers we hear little or nothing.

The men were worse than the officers. Instead of the sturdy agricultural labourers and farmers' sons that filled the ranks of the King's regiments, they were 'the refuse of the vilest employments in London,' as Orme described them fifty years later; 'the worst of their kind,' according to Clive. Of all nationalities, ages, and colours, badly armed, badly fed, and badly paid, they were almost without discipline.

The native chiefs vied with each other in getting Europeans into their service, so that none but the most wretched would stay to serve the Company. At the best they were only factory guards, and maintained for purposes of escort and display; and it was always the Company's practice to retain officers and men in their service up to any age.

On one occasion we find Boone writing to the directors that 'it would not do to disgust the men too much.' Miserable as was their pay of sixteen *laris*[9] a month, we find them complaining to the council that Midford had kept back two *laris* a month from each man. To which Midford replied that he never received nor took any more profit from the soldiers than what other officers did, all through the island of Bombay; with which answer the council was apparently satisfied.

The real grievance of the men appears to have been that Midford, not being a military officer, was not entitled to make the deduction. The directors were careful in enjoining that powder was not to be wasted at exercise; "but sometimes the men must be used to firing, lest in time of action they should start at the noise or the recoil of their arms." To bring such officers and men into the field was to invite disaster. Soldiers are not made by dressing men in uniform and putting muskets into their hands.

---

9. The *lari* was the well-known hook money of the Persian Gulf. It was worth about sixpence.

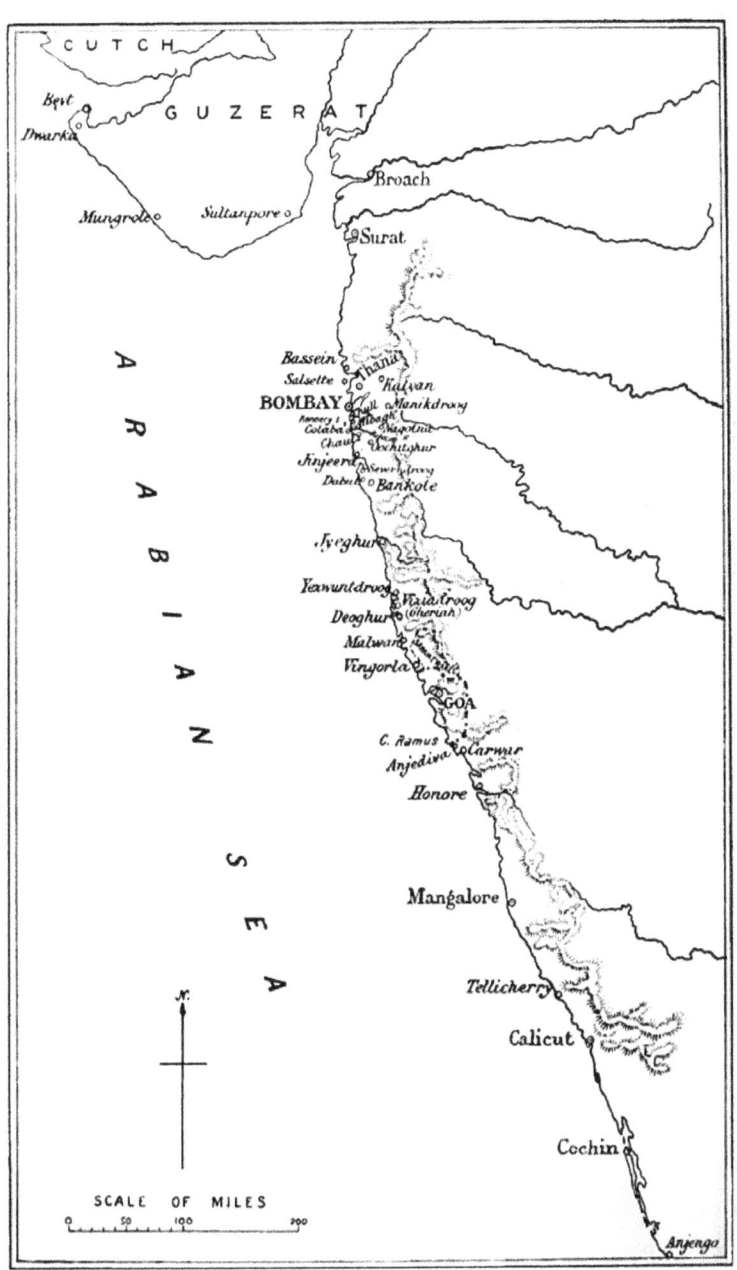

Chapter 6

Expedition Against Kennery

The islet of Kennery, about ten miles from the mouth of the harbour, and three from the mainland, had long been a thorn in the side of Bombay trade. At the time of the first occupation of Bombay it was uninhabited. In 1679 it was suddenly occupied by Sivajee, who began to fortify it. The danger of this to Bombay was at once seen, and part of the garrison was sent in small vessels, afterwards reinforced by the *Revenge*, frigate, to intercept the communication between Kennery and the mainland. On the 18th October, the Mahratta fleet bore down and engaged. In half an hour the *Dove*, grab, hauled down its colours and was captured, and all the smaller vessels made sail for Bombay, leaving the *Revenge*, like its more famous namesake, alone amidst its foes. Fortunately, there were on board two sturdy Englishmen, Minchin, the Company's commodore, and Keigwin, the commander of the garrison.

Undismayed by the odds against them, Minchin and Keigwin gallantly fought their ship; all attempts at boarding were repelled with loss, five of the Mahratta *gallivats* were sunk, and, at last, the whole Mahratta fleet took to flight, pursued by the *Revenge*, and sought refuge in the shallow waters at the mouth of the Negotna River. Two days later, they came out again, but found Keigwin and Minchin so ready to engage, that they desisted from the attempt to reach Kennery. In this way, for some time, a partial blockade of the Negotna River was maintained by the *Revenge*, which had been reinforced by the *Hunter* frigate, and a number of small vessels from Bombay.

In spite of all efforts, a few Mahratta vessels from time to time evaded the blockade, and kept Kennery supplied with provisions and arms. This unexpected opposition from a company of traders stirred Sivajee to settle the matter by an attack on Bombay, which was in no condition to make any resistance. He marched five thousand men to Kalyan, and demanded permission, of the Portuguese, to land at Thana and march on Bombay. The permission was refused, but the Bombay Council were so alarmed lest the Portuguese should ultimately give way, that they opened negotiations with Sivajee.

Meanwhile, his seizure of Kennery had alarmed the *Seedee*, who sent his fleet into Bombay harbour, and offered his co-operation to the President, who accepted it with some misgivings. Before long, it was discovered that the *Seedee* intended to keep Kennery for himself, if he could capture it, which seemed to the council as bad as if it were in Sivajee's hands, so the English squadron held aloof, while the struggle for Kennery continued between the *Seedee* and the *Mahrattas*. Sivajee was too much occupied with other matters to trouble about Bombay, and in March, 1680, a treaty of peace was made. His struggle with the *Seedee* for the possession of Kennery went on, with results that are not recorded; but eventually both parties appear to have left the place to itself. In 1710, Conajee Angria seized the islet and fortified it.

By the end of October all was ready. The ships from England, with the merchandise and money for the yearly investment, had arrived, and joined in the expedition. In order to put an end to the quarrels among commanders that had marked the failure of former expeditions, Boone resolved to take the command himself; so, on the 1st November, he hoisted his flag on board the *Addison*, East Indiaman, having with him Mr. Walter Brown and other factors and writers. There was at this time in the service a renegade Portuguese, one Manuel de Castro, who had been in Angria's service before Boone had given him employment. He had been present at Hamilton's attack on Carwar, when his misbehaviour had been such as to make all present distrust him. By his boasts of his knowledge of Angria's harbours he had gained the confidence of the council, and had been appointed commodore of the Company's *gallivats*.

But several of the English captains refused to serve under him, protesting that they knew his character better than the governor did; so Boone contented himself by giving him command of only five *gallivats*. On the 2nd, the squadron weighed anchor, and, on the following day anchored off Kennery. It consisted of the *Addison* and *Dartmouth*, East Indiamen, the *Victoria* frigate, the *Revenge* and *Defiance* grabs, the *Fame* galley, the *Hunter ketch*, two bomb-*ketches*, and forty-eight gallivats. On the 6th they were joined by the *Morrice*, and on the 12th by the *Stanhope*, East Indiamen. Directly after anchoring, a futile bombardment was opened on the Kennery fort, but the distance was so great that nothing was effected but waste of ammunition. The ships then stood in closer, and opened fire again, while the *Dartmouth* ran in and fired several broadsides. While this was going on, the *Victory* and *Revenge* were signalled to attack two *grabs* that were seen coming out of the harbour; but, on fourteen *gallivats* coming out to assist the *grabs*, they were recalled. The 4th was spent in preparations for a landing, and the *gallivats* rowed round the island to choose a landing-place.

It was finally arranged that the soldiers and marines should land to windward, while the *sepoys*, covered by the fire of *grabs* and *gallivats*, should land at the opposite side of the island, to leeward. But when the moment arrived, next morning, the *sepoys* absolutely refused to land, in spite of the severest measures.[1] The soldiers and marines, three hundred in number, landed, but were beaten back with a loss of eighteen killed and fifty wounded, "more by ye force of stones hoven from ye rocks than fier arms." Some loss was occasioned by the bursting of a gun on board one of the *gallivats*. Manuel de Castro, with his squadron of *gallivats*, had been ordered to lie off the mouth of the harbour and prevent reinforcements reaching Kennery. Notwithstanding, he allowed five of Angria's *gallivats* to slip in with ammunition and provisions for the besieged, of which they were believed to stand much in need.

The 6th was occupied in making preparations for another attack, and volunteers were called for from among the sailors, for which service they were to receive forty *rupees* each, which, at the existing rate of exchange, was reckoned equal to five pounds sterling. The loss of a leg or arm was to be recompensed by a sum of £30 on return to England, and employment for life under the Company. The married men were promised, if killed, that their widows should receive £30, with £10 for each child. These offers procured some forty volunteers, who were to be led by Gideon Russell, mate of the *Morrice*.

Early next morning the attacking party were put into the boats, to land under cover of the fire of the *Britannia*, *Fame* and *Revenge*; when it was found that a strong current prevented disembarkation, and the boats were forced to lie off under a heavy fire, until the tide changed. To make matters worse, Manuel de Castro ran two of his *gallivats* ashore under the guns of the castle, so that fifty or sixty men were killed or wounded before a landing was effected. At ten o'clock the boats pulled for the landing-place; but the tide was still running

---

1. "Killed and wounded several of them, but all to no purpose."—*Log of the Addison*.

so strongly that they were thrown into confusion, and many of the attacking party never landed at all. The *sepoys* again refused to land.

A small party of seamen, headed by Gideon Russell, attacked the gateway under a shower of shot and stones, and, before long, Russell fell, grievously wounded. He was carried back to the *Morrice*, where he died next day. The seamen continued their attack under Clement Downing, backed by Major Stanton, Captain Coxsidge, and the soldiers. John Steele, the carpenter's mate of the *Morrice*, with his broad axe hewed at the gate and nearly effected an entrance, when the cowardice of two of Stanton's captains caused the attack to miscarry. One of them threw down his sword, which was carried to Boone, who, on return to Bombay, ordered him to be broke at the head of the garrison.

The other, somewhat more courageous, came boldly up to the gate and fired his pistol; but the bullet rebounded and struck him on the nose; upon which he ordered the drums to beat a retreat, and the soldiers got back to the boats, leaving a small handful of seamen to prosecute the attack. These, in turn, seeing the hopelessness of any further attempts, retreated to their boats, and rowed off under a heavy fire, leaving many wounded to be massacred by the enemy. It was the old story, repeated so often on these occasions; a badly planned attack carried out half-heartedly by undisciplined men, under one or two resolute leaders; as soon as the leaders were disabled, the rest retreated with more or less loss.

A desultory bombardment was continued for some days, and some shots were fired against Colaba; but Kennery was now well provided with ammunition, and could return two shots for every one fired by the Bombay squadron. On the 11th, Angria sent a flag of truce to offer terms, which were rejected. On the 14th, Boone returned to Bombay in the *Dartmouth*, seeing that nothing more could be effected, and, on the 24th, the whole squadron made sail for Bombay, after exhausting all their ammunition. Their return seems to have been hastened by the appearance of Angria's fleet from Gheriah, which had Bombay for a time at its mercy.

The failure of the attack on Kennery, under his own eyes, taught Boone that, without some assistance from England, he could hope to accomplish little against Angria, whose ships now lay off the harbour, making it difficult for trading vessels to go in or out. Three times the *Morrice* got under way, and three times had to return, before she could start on her return voyage to Europe. In consequence of Boone's representations, the directors sent out the *St. George*, a sixty-gun ship, to act as a guardship for the harbour. Her arrival only served to show the incompetency of many of the Company's naval officers at that time. In laying the ship on shore to scour its bottom after the voyage from England, its back was broken, and the *St. George* became a total wreck.

Meanwhile, with an eye to a future campaign against Angria's strongholds, Boone set to work to build a floating battery. The *Phram*, as it was called, was designed with shot-proof sides to carry twelve 48-pdrs.; but, as will appear before long, its fate was as ignominious as that of the *St. George*.

His own observation had convinced Boone of the treachery of Manuel de Castro. On his return to Bombay, the renegade was put in irons, and shipped off to St. Helena. There he was detected in fomenting a mutiny among the convicts and slaves. He was deported, and before long made his way back into Angria's service.

Meanwhile, the wall round the town, the building of which had been one of Boone's earliest projects, was nearing completion. It was built entirely, or almost entirely, by contributions from the native merchants, and Boone reported to the directors that, when the whole space was built over, the ground-rents would realize *Rs.*8890 a year for the Company's treasury. The church also, the building of which had been started by Aislabie, was finished about this time. The original chapel inside the factory was no longer able to accommodate the increasing English population, besides being in a ruinous condition.

Like other chiefs along the coast, the Bombay authorities gave passes to traders living under their protection, and in their warfare with Angria they had adopted the practice of other chiefs, of not recognizing the immunity of vessels that did not carry passes from themselves. We find at this time the Kattiawar traders complaining of two ships having been seized that held protective passes from Angria. In reply they were told that they must have English passes. The Company was at war with Angria, and his power was increased by those who paid him for protection. So, like all neutrals, they had to suffer in a war with which they had no concern.

Apprehensive of a fresh attack after the monsoon, Angria opened delusive negotiations for a treaty of peace, through his feudal lord, Sahoojee. Boone was regularly taken in, and announced with satisfaction, to the directors, that a treaty had been made, under which Angria contracted to restore all ships and vessels he had taken, except the *Suc-*

cess, which was hopelessly decayed, for which he was to pay *Rs*.10,000, or to restore goods to that amount. In lieu of captured cargoes he was to pay Rs.50,000, or to give goods of equal value, and within two years he was to pay *Rs*.10,000 more, for which payment Sahoojee undertook to be surety.

Boone reported that he had captured from Angria prizes to the value of *Rs*.9785, which, together with the above payment, and a two-*per-cent*. war-tax on the people of Bombay, would go some way to recoup the Company for their losses and the cost of the expeditions. Altogether, the prospects of increased trade were brighter, but, so long as Angria held Colaba, he considered there could be no permanent peace. He was soon undeceived. As soon as Angria saw that he was safe from attack for another season, he repudiated the treaty, and by the beginning of the new year his piratical doings were renewed.

CHAPTER 7

Expedition Against Gheriah

In addition to other embarrassments, Boone became involved, at this time, in a quarrel with the Portuguese. The surrender of Bombay to the English had, from the first, been extremely distasteful to the Goa authorities, who understood the value of the place better than did the authorities in Lisbon; and they had so interpreted the treaty that gave Bombay to the English that, at the time of transfer, they had managed to retain everything except the island of Bombay. The English had been obliged to renounce all claim to Salsette and other dependencies of Bombay, or to exclusive possession of the harbour, and to agree that the Portuguese residents should be exempted from the payment of customs, and have full liberty of trade with the Portuguese establishments in Salsette.

This last condition had been repudiated in England, but continued to be claimed by the Portuguese, who harassed the position of the English by levying duties, and impeding the passage of supplies, while they gave asylum to deserters and runaways of all kinds. By the treaty, toleration for the exercise of the Roman Catholic religion had been secured; and there had remained in Bombay a large establishment of Franciscan friars, who made no efforts to conceal their hostility to the Company's government. In addition to other treacherous acts, Boone had to complain of the friars tampering with his soldiers and slaves, and encouraging them to desert.

In order to put an end to the evil, he banished all the Portuguese friars, and installed in their place an Italian bishop and some Italian Carmelite friars. This was held by the Goa authorities to be an infringement of the rights of the king of Portugal. In retaliation, all Roman Catholics in Bombay were forbidden to recognize the authority of the Italian bishop and friars, and the Portuguese General of the North was ordered to prohibit all intercourse with Bombay, and to inflict the severest penalties on all persons attempting to go there or to leave it.

Those who are captured shall be whipped and put in the galleys for five years, and, if of noble birth, they shall pay the sum of one thousand *xeraphims* in lieu of working in the galleys, and shall be transported for five years to the fortress of Diu.[1]

It seemed as if Boone was to have a Portuguese war added to his other troubles. Fortunately, more moderate counsels prevailed, and, in September, a conciliatory letter was written to Boone by the Viceroy, announcing his approaching departure. A few days later, the new Viceroy, Francisco José de Sampaio e Castro, arrived in Goa. While the quarrel was in progress, a native ship from Surat, bound for Jeddah, was captured off Bassein by a European pirate ship. This was probably England's ship, *Victory*, of which we shall hear more directly. The ship and cargo, valued at twelve *lakhs*, were carried off, and the passengers and crew put ashore at Malabar Hill.

A month later, Boone received intelligence of a serious loss to the Company's trade from the Madagascar pirates. On the 7th August, the *Greenwich*, Captain Kirby, and the *Cassandra*, Captain James Macrae, bringing the usual yearly investment for Bombay and Surat, were in Johanna roads, engaged in watering. At anchor, near them, was an Ostend ship that had called for the same purpose. A few days before, they had received intelligence that a French pirate, Oliver la Bouche,[2] had run on a reef off Mayotta, and lost his ship, and was engaged in building a new one. Thinking that the opportunity of catching the pirates at a disadvantage should not be lost, Macrae and Kirby agreed to go in search of them and attack them. They had just completed their arrangements when two strange sails hove in sight. They proved to be the *Victory*, a French-built ship of forty-six guns, commanded by the well-known pirate, Edward England, and the *Fancy*, a Dutch-built ship of twenty-four guns, commanded by Taylor.

Macrae and Kirby prepared to give them a hot reception, the Ostend ship promising to stand by them. So far were they from simply

---

1. Proclamation issued at Goa, 19th July, 1720 (Danvers).
2. This was Oliver Levasseur, otherwise La Buze of Calais, a noted French pirate. By the English he was called La Bouche, and, in one ship's log, Lepouse. On Woodes Rogers assuming the governorship of the Bahamas, La Bouche and England sailed for Madagascar.

trying to make their escape, that they looked forward to the handsome reward the Company would give them for the capture of the pirates. From what followed it is easy to see that Macrae's was the guiding spirit in this. Cables were cut, and they stood out to sea, but, owing to the light baffling winds, made little way. By next morning the pirates had closed, and bore down with a black flag (skull and crossbones) at the main, a red flag at the fore, and the cross of St. George at the ensign staff. The *Greenwich* and the Ostender, having a better wind than the *Cassandra*, had got some distance away. In vain Macrae fired gun after gun at the *Greenwich* to make Kirby heave to. In a most dastardly way the captain of the *Greenwich* pursued his course, taking the Ostender with him, till he had got well to windward; when, at a distance of two or three miles, he hove to and watched the fate of the *Cassandra*.

The *Cassandra* was a new ship of 380 tons, on her first voyage. Macrae was a thoroughly good seaman, with a fine crew that were attached to him, and was resolved to fight his ship to the last. Early in the engagement he gave the *Victory* some shots between wind and water, which made England keep off till he had stopped the leaks. Taylor got out the boats of the *Fancy* and tried to tow her alongside, to carry the *Cassandra* by boarding, but such good practice was made by the *Cassandra's* marksmen that the design was given up. At the end of three hours the *Victory* had repaired damages, and was closing again. Macrae had lost so many of his crew, that, giving up all hope of assistance from Kirby, he determined to run his ship ashore. The *Fancy*, which drew less water, followed with the intention of boarding, but got aground within pistol-shot, with her bows towards the *Cassandra's* broadside, and the action recommenced hotter than ever.

There the two ships lay, both fast aground, pelting each other furiously, till the crew of the *Fancy*, finding the *Cassandra's* fire too hot for them, left their guns and ran below. Had Kirby come to his assistance at this moment, Macrae's triumph would have been assured; but this was the moment chosen by Kirby to bear up and shape his course for Bombay. England in the *Victory*, seeing that the *Greenwich* might be disregarded, sent three boats full of men to reinforce the *Fancy*; by which time there had been so many killed and wounded on board the *Cassandra*, that the crew, losing heart, refused to fight the ship any longer. Thirteen had been killed and twenty-four wounded, among the latter Macrae himself, who had been struck by a musket ball on the head; so, some in the long boat and some by swimming reached the shore, leaving on board three wounded men who could not be moved, and who were butchered by the pirates.

Not deeming it safe to linger on the coast, Macrae and his crew hastened inland, reaching the town of the local chief, twenty-five miles off, the following morning. Exhausted with fatigue and wounds, almost naked, they were in a pitiable condition. The natives received them hospitably, supplied their wants to the best of their ability, and refused to surrender them to the pirates, who offered a reward for them.

After the first rage of the pirates, at the heavy losses they had sustained, had abated, and soothed, no doubt, by the capture of a fine new ship with £75,000 on board in hard cash, Macrae ventured to open communications with them. Several among them had sailed with him, and his reputation for considerate treatment of his men was well known. With all their faults, they were not all of them men to resent greatly, after their first fury had cooled, the loss that had been suffered in fair fight; so England gave him a promise of safety, and he ventured himself among them. The *Cassandra* and the *Fancy* had been floated, and Macrae was entertained on board his own ship with his own liquors and provisions. His position was not without danger, as there were many brutal fellows among the pirates. England, who had a reputation for good treatment of prisoners, befriended him; but Taylor, whose influence was greatest among the most brutal of the rovers, insisted he should be made an end of.

In the midst of the quarrel, a fierce-looking fellow with a wooden leg and his belt full of pistols, intervened, asking with many oaths for Macrae, who thought his last moment had come.[3] He was pleasantly surprised when the ruffian took him by the hand, and swore with many oaths that he would make mince-meat of the first man that hurt him; and protested, with more oaths, that Macrae was an honest fellow, and he had formerly sailed with him. So the dispute ended. Taylor was plied with punch till he was prevailed on to consent that the *Fancy*, together with some of the *Cassandra's* cargo, should be given to Macrae, and before he could recover from his carouse, Macrae had got safe to shore again.

As soon as the pirates had left the coast, in the *Victory* and the *Cas-*

---

3. Stevenson, in *Treasure Island*, evidently took his idea of John Silver, the one-legged pirate, from this incident. "Now what a ship was christened" (he makes him say) "so let her stay, I says. So it was with the *Cassandra* as brought us all home from Malabar, after England took the Viceroy of the Indies. . . . First with England, then with Flint; that's my story."

sandra, Macrae set to work to patch up the much-battered *Fancy*, and in a few days sailed for Bombay, with forty-one of his ship's company, among whom were two passengers and twelve soldiers. After forty-eight days of terrible sufferings almost naked, half starved, and reduced to a daily pint of water each, they reached Bombay on the 26th October. It would have been well for the Company if they had had more captains like Macrae. His arrival brought much obloquy on Kirby, whose shameful desertion was now made known.

The pirates only detained one of the *Cassandra's* crew—Richard Lazenby, the carpenter's mate, whom they forced unwillingly to go with them. There is still extant a curious account by Lazenby of his cruise with the pirates. He tells of the cruel tortures inflicted on all captured natives; how on the Malabar coast they had friends, especially among the Dutch at Cochin, who bought their plunder, supplied them with provisions, and gave them information of armed ships to be avoided, and rich prizes to be intercepted. Those who wished to retire from the trade were given passages to Europe with their ill-gotten gains, in French ships; and finally, after witnessing the capture of the Portuguese Viceroy, to be related presently, he was put ashore at Bourbon, whence, in time, he made his way to England.

Since the renewal of war by Angria, at the beginning of the year, Boone had resolved to strike another blow against Gheriah, and all through the monsoon preparations had been made for action in September. Great things were expected of the *Phram*, which was, however, not ready when the expedition sailed. The direction of affairs was, on this occasion, entrusted to Mr. Walter Brown, who was styled for the occasion "Admiral of the Fleet, and commander-in-chief of all the forces." On the 13th September anchor was weighed, and on the morning of the 19th they arrived off Gheriah. At Dabul, where they had called in for news, they learned that the *Phram* and the *Chandos* might soon be expected, but that there was no prospect of Captain Johnson's machine being ready to take part in the expedition.

What Captain Johnson's machine was we do not learn, but the intelligence 'mightily disconcerted the soldiery.' The squadron consisted of the *London*, which acted as flagship, the *Victory* frigate, the *Revenge* and *Defiance* grabs, the *Hunter* galley, two *gallivats*, a bomb-ketch, a fire-ship, and a number of fishing-boats for landing troops. The troops for the expedition consisted of 350 soldiers and *topasses* and 80 chosen *sepoys*. Brown appears to have been thoroughly incompetent for such a command, and the undertaking was destined to add one more to the dismal list of failures. His first act was to make the *London* exchange useless shots with the fort at a mile distance. The following day, the bomb-*ketch* was ordered to run close in within pistol-shot, and bombard the place at night. One shell and one carcass were fired, neither of which went halfway, by reason of the mortars being so faultily constructed that the chambers could not contain a sufficient charge of powder. 'This misfortune set the people a-grumbling.'

On the 21st, Brown held a consultation of his officers, and proposed to land three hundred men, at night, a mile from the town, so as to surprise it at daylight. The officers protested against the scheme; they justly remarked that it would be folly to make such an attack before the arrival of the whole force. The *Phram* and the *Chandos*, with the platoons of Europeans, were still to come. They represented that the garrison of the fort alone was a thousand strong, to say nothing of the small walled town which must be taken before the fort could be attacked. Such a proposal was not likely to increase their confidence in Brown. Sickness had already set in among the troops, and that evening Captain Jeremiah Easthope died of fever. Brown was all for immediate action, without having any definite plan.

On the 22nd, Gordon was ordered to land with fifty men, and occupy a small building on the top of a hill on the north side of the river. What he was expected to do there does not appear. Soon, a number of boats full of men were observed crossing from the fort to engage Gordon, so a reinforcement of fifty men was sent to him. On reaching the hill, Gordon found that what had been taken for a building consisted only of a natural pile of loose stones, such as are to be frequently seen on the Deccan hills, and there was nothing for it but to re-embark. He managed his retreat to the landing-place in good order, followed by the enemy at musket-shot distance. Several times he faced about, but the enemy always shrank from close quarters.

Nothing had been done to cover the place of embarkation, and it was only after the strongest remonstrances from those on board that Brown was prevailed on to order the *Revenge* and the *Hunter* to stand in and cover the re-embarkation of Gordon's party. In spite of this precaution, a lieutenant, a sergeant, a quartermaster of the *London* and six men were killed, and about twenty men wounded. It is difficult to imagine anything feebler and more aimless than the whole proceeding.

The next day the bomb-*ketch* was again sent in to bombard the fort, with the same result as before. The proceedings were enlivened by the punishment of Sergeant Passmore, who was reported by Gordon for cowardly behaviour. He was sent round the fleet to receive ten lashes alongside each ship. The next three days were spent in idleness, awaiting the *Phram*, from which so much was expected. On board ship there was no discipline, but plenty of hard drinking. In order to make the men fight well, Brown's idea was to supply them with unlimited rum: the officers kept pace with the men in their libations, and what little discipline existed soon disappeared. Orders were disobeyed, while drunkenness, violence, and insubordination reigned unchecked. When remonstrances were addressed to Brown, he refused to stop the supply of liquor, saying that the people must not be put out of humour at this juncture, and they must drink as they pleased: all which is duly recorded by Captain Upton of the *London*. The enemy meanwhile was observed busily constructing new batteries, and boats full of armed men were constantly crossing the river, but nothing was done to intercept them.

At last, the *Chandos*, *Pelham*, and *Phram* arrived, having spent ten days in their voyage from Bombay. Nothing better occurred to Brown than to send the *Phram* at once to engage the fort. On opening fire, it was found that her ports were so low and the gun-carriages so high, that her guns could only be fired when depressed so as to strike the water twenty yards off. So she was brought out again with one man mortally wounded, and the officers and soldiers so mightily discouraged that they declared, unless she could be made serviceable, it was useless to attempt anything further. The ships' carpenters were set to work on the *Phram*, while the dejection and drinking increased. Fifty men of the *Chandos* who had not yet had an opportunity of gauging Brown's incapacity, volunteered, for forty *rupees* a head, to join a landing party; but not a single seaman in the squadron would consent, 'upon any consideration whatsoever,' to go on board the *Phram*, till an increased bounty secured the services of the *Chandos'* sailors.

By the 29th all was ready for the grand attack. Two landing parties, one of three hundred and forty soldiers under Captain Stanton, and the other of two hundred and thirty-seven seamen under Captain Woodward, were held in readiness, and soon after midday the fleet stood into the inner harbour, with the exception of the *Phram*, which engaged the fort from the outer harbour. Lieutenant Wise had been selected as a fit person to command and point the *Phram's* guns, which he did so badly that his shot mostly fell in the inner harbour. The Mahrattas were quite ready for them, and all the afternoon the cannonade went on, till sunset put an end to it. Five men on board the *Phram* were wounded, but it had engaged at too great a distance to do or suffer much harm.

Brown, in the *London*, had kept out of action, and contented himself with sending six dozen of wine and arrack to the men on board the *Phram*, together with orders to Stanton, who was on board, to warp into the harbour at night and renew the action next morning. The following day firing recommenced, and it was found necessary to displace Lieutenant Wise, he being continually drunk, and to allow the sailors to point their own guns. The closer range caused numerous casualties on board the *Phram*. Among the soldiers, Mr. Tuladay and four men were killed, and a great number wounded. The seamen also had several killed and wounded. Many of the casualties were caused by the bursting of a gun on board the *Phram*. The explosion fired the gun on the opposite side of the deck, which was loaded with grape, and pointing over a boat full of *topasses*. The flame from the gun ignited their cartridge boxes, and the poor wretches were terribly scorched and injured.

The fire of the ships in the inner harbour was successful in destroying a number of Angria's ships that had sought refuge in the river; one of five hundred tons, one of two hundred tons, and ten smaller ones were set on fire and burnt. By nightfall, all hands thought they had done enough, and told Stanton so, and in spite of Brown's messages of expostulation, they took advantage of a land breeze to come out. At midnight came Captain Woodward, of the *Revenge*, to report, in a panic, to Brown that he had left his ship on the rocks close to the fort, and that both vessel and crew were as good as lost. Half an hour after, the *Revenge* was seen coming out with the other vessels. She had not been ashore at all, and the only conclusion was that Woodward was frightened out of his senses; so he was put in irons for his cowardice.

Thus came to an end the grand attack, and nothing better was to be expected. "I have continual disturbances in the ship dayly by the officers excessive drinking, and noe manner of command carryed," wrote Captain Upton, of the *London*. A few days later he records how Captain S. and Mr. D.[4] fought with their fists in the roundhouse before Mr. Brown, who took no notice of it.

The next few days were spent in repairing damages. While thus employed, messengers came from the Kempsant, offering to join hands with the English in attacking Angria. A quarrel had arisen between the

---

4. Probably Stanton and Drage.

two chiefs, owing to Angria having plundered some of the Kempsant's ships. But he stipulated that Angria's fort at Deoghur, seven leagues to the south, should be first attacked; so, on the 7th October, part of the fleet was sent down to reconnoitre.

On the 16th, fresh stores of *arrack*, water and provisions having been received from Goa, Brown called a consultation of the officers on board the *Addison*, and proposed another landing under the *Phrams* guns. But the officers were disheartened, undisciplined, and under no control. One objection after another was raised, and the council of war came to an end by other officers of the squadron, who had learned what was going on, coming aboard, and conveying to Brown in no measured terms that they would have nothing to do with it. One of them in a passion told Brown he was mad, and did not know what he was about—which was true enough. The next day, a foolish show of landing was made, and then Brown decided to abandon the attempt and transfer his attack to Deoghur.

Deoghur, or, as it was sometimes called, Tamana, was one of the ten principal forts ceded to Angria in 1713. It commanded the small but good harbour formed by the Tamana River. This was Angria's southernmost stronghold. The name Tamana is still to be found at a small place ten miles up the river. Here Brown brought his squadron on the 18th October. The usual desultory and harmless bombardment followed; the *Phram* and the bomb-*ketch* being equally inefficient. Then, when Brown suggested a landing party to storm the place, the officers refused to second him, and so, with some additional loss, the attack on Deoghur came to an end. Not a word is said as to any assistance rendered by the Kempsant. At daybreak on the 21st, the whole squadron sailed northward, but the tale of Brown's incompetency was not complete.

A little before noon next morning four strange sails were seen in the offing, which, before long, were made out to be the dreaded Madagascar pirates, with the *Cassandra*, *Victory*, and two prizes they had just taken. The sight of them struck Brown with terror, though a little reflection would have shown him that the pirates would have little or no inducement to attack armed ships carrying no valuable merchandise. He directed his whole squadron to anchor off Gheriah, which must have appeared puzzling to his late antagonists in that place. Hoping to evade the pirate ships, anchor was weighed in the night, and the squadron sailed northward, no order being preserved, and the fleet getting much scattered.

As it happened, the pirates had mistaken them for Angria's fleet, and were standing to the northward in search of prey, without any thought of attacking them. Without any hostile intention on either side, the two squadrons became intermingled. While it was still dark, the party on the *London* was startled by a cannon shot flying over them, and in the faint morning light they saw a large ship on their quarter. On hailing to ask her name, an answer came back that it was the *Victory*. Brown preferred to believe that it was his own ship of that name; but his answering hail, giving the name of the *London*, was replied to with a broadside, to which a smart fire was returned by the *Revenge* and the *Defiance*, that were close astern.

On both sides there was no willingness to fight. The pirates were at first seized with consternation at discovering their mistake; they had turned their prizes adrift after throwing their sails overboard, and, with only three hundred men for their joint crews, forty of them negroes, were not strong enough to engage the Bombay squadron. But England was a man who preferred fighting to running, so putting a bold face on the matter, the *Cassandra* ran through the fleet, firing into the *Victory*, the *Chandos*, and the *Phram*. The *Chandos*, which was towing the *Phram*, at once cast it loose. The fleet scattered in all directions, like a flock of sheep when a strange dog runs through it. Upton, of the *London*, a chicken-hearted fellow, persuaded Brown that they ought not to engage, as Boone had sent them to attack Gheriah, but had given them no instructions about the Madagascar pirates.

Brown seemingly did not want much persuading, and crowded all sail to escape; at the same time striking his flag to show that he did not intend fighting, which excited the indignation of his own sailors and the derision of the pirates. He next sent orders by a *gallivat* for the *Phram* to be burned, and thus that useless machine, from which so much had been expected; and that had cost so much money and labour, came to an end.

These foolish proceedings gave England the measure of his antagonists. 'Observing the indifferency of the fleet,' the best way of saving himself was, he thought, to 'play the Bull-beggar' with them; so he set to work to chase them northward. The superior sailing powers of the pirates enabled them to do as they pleased.

When they overtook the rearmost of the ships Brown had still got with him, they backed their sails and fired into them till they had got well ahead again. In this ignominious fashion the greater part of the fleet was shuffled along for two days by the pirates, as a flock of sheep is driven by a couple of sheep-dogs, till they at last found refuge in Goa. The soldiers on board the *London* improved the occasion by breaking into the '*Lazaretto*' and getting drunk on the wine they found there. Part of the fleet made for Carwar, and others found safety under the guns of Anjediva. The pirates, having effected their purpose of driving them off, turned south and took the *Elizabeth* at anchor off Honore.

Before long, an indignant letter from Boone ordered Brown to cruise southward and engage the pirates at all hazards; so the unhappy Brown put to sea again. The news of the capture of the *Elizabeth* was enough for him: on the third day he turned northward again and made for Bombay; to make his peace with the exasperated governor as he best could. It is not difficult to imagine Boone's disgust at the failure of his schemes, and the worthlessness of those he had to depend upon; but it must be admitted that these desultory attacks, first on one place and then on another, were not calculated to effect anything useful. Had he concentrated his efforts on Kennery, he might have rendered the waters of Bombay more secure.

Brown laid the blame of his failure on the disobedience of his officers, which had been so flagrant as to conceal his own incapacity; so, on the 12th December, Boone again despatched him to search for the pirates, and give protection to the country vessels bringing up pepper from the southern factories. He took with him a fine squadron: the *Greenwich*, 42 guns; the *Chandos*, 40 guns; the *Victory*, 26 guns; the *Britannia*, 24 guns; the *Revenge*, 16 guns; and a fireship. The pusillanimous Upton was left behind, and, next to himself in command of the expedition, but in reality the moving spirit, he took the gallant Macrae. England and Taylor had meanwhile been constrained to run down to the Laccadives, for want of water and provisions.

Not getting what they wanted, they had come northward again to Cochin, where they were royally entertained by the Dutch authorities. They were supplied with everything they required, including a present, from the governor, of a boat loaded with arrack, and sixty bales of sugar, for all of which handsome payment was made, while handfuls of *duccatoons* were thrown into the boat for the boatmen to scramble for. A fine clock and gold watch, found in the *Cassandra* when captured, were sent as a present to the governor's daughter, and formal salutes were fired on both sides as they entered and left the harbour. No wonder that they were made welcome along the coast.

On leaving Cochin, they took a small vessel from Tellicherry sailing under a Bombay pass. From the master they learned that the Bombay squadron, with Macrae in command, was cruising in search of them. They were roused to fury by this news of Macrae's 'ingratitude,' and vied with each other in devising the tortures to which they would subject him if he fell into their hands again, while their anger was vented on England and all who had stood up for Macrae after the capture of the *Cassandra*. Before long they were sighted by Brown, who bore down on them and signalled them to heave to. This behaviour, so different from their previous experiences, was little to their liking. They made sail for the southwards, and, for two days, were held in chase, till by superior sailing they lost their pursuers.

Such an extraordinary change in the behaviour of the Bombay squadron taught them that the Indian coast was no longer a safe place for honest rovers. It was expedient to take themselves elsewhere: so sail was made for Mauritius. Against Macrae their curses were loud and deep. A villain they had treated so well as to give him a ship and other presents, and now to be in arms against them! No fate was bad enough for such a man. They had been cruelly deceived. To appease their wrath they turned upon England. But for his foolish championship of Macrae, this would not have happened. Taylor had been right all along. They would only follow him in future. In their rage they first talked of hanging England, till more moderate counsels prevailed, and it was decided to maroon him at Mauritius, which was done. England and three others who had befriended Macrae were set on shore, among them, no doubt, the one-legged pirate, and in due course of time made their way over to St. Mary's.[5]

At St. Mary's the command of the *Victory* was made over to Oliver La Bouche, or La Buze, whose efforts at shipbuilding had apparently not met with success, and the two ships, in company, before long took what was probably the richest prize that ever fell into pirate hands. The ex-viceroy of Goa, the Conde de Ericeira, had sailed for Lisbon, in January, in the *Nostra Senhora de Cabo*, a seventy-gun ship, taking with him a rich consignment of jewels for the Portuguese government, and the proceeds of his own private trading during the three years of his viceroyalty. Off the Cape they encountered a heavy storm, which dismasted the ship, forced them to throw many of their guns overboard, and obliged them to put back to Bourbon to refit.

Taylor and La Buze, learning the helplessness of the viceroy's ship,

---

5. In Lazenby's narrative, England is mentioned as Seegar, which was probably his real name, England being only an *alias*.

sailed into the anchorage under English colours. A salute from the viceroy's ship was answered with a shotted broadside, and, in the confusion that ensued, the Portuguese ship was boarded and carried almost without resistance. Seldom or never had such a prize fallen into pirate hands so easily. The booty in diamonds and money was in the shape most coveted by the rovers. The jewels alone were estimated at over three million dollars. The hard cash was said to be five hundred thousand crowns, and the viceroy was forced to raise another two thousand crowns as a personal ransom, which would have been higher, had he not convinced them that part of the jewels and money on board was his own property.

Bourbon was a French possession, but the governor, M. Desforges, was obliged to observe *une grande circonspection* in his dealings with the pirates who came and went as they pleased. Bernardin de St. Pierre, who visited Bourbon nearly fifty years later, repeats a tradition, how La Buze sat at table between the viceroy and the governor, and in an access of generosity remitted the viceroy's ransom. He further tells us that La Buze eventually settled down in the island, and was hung some years later.

Taylor, continuing his cruise in the *Cassandra*, took a fine Ostend ship, and carried her to St. Mary's. While most of the pirates were on shore, the prisoners overpowered the few left to guard them, and carried off the ship. We get a last glimpse of the *Cassandra* in a private letter written to the directors in May, 1723, from Jamaica, in which it is stated that the *Cassandra* was lying at Portobello, while Taylor was engaged in negotiating with the captain of an English man-of-war for a pardon. The negotiations apparently fell through, as Taylor was eventually given a commission by the Spaniards. The letter relates how the crew boasted that they had, each man, twelve hundred pounds in gold and silver, besides a great store of diamonds and many rich goods. Of the sharing of these diamonds, Johnson tells a story how one man, being given for his share one big diamond instead of a number of small ones, broke it up with a hammer, so that he might have as many 'sparks' as the others.

Macrae's defence of the *Cassandra*, and the boldness and ability he displayed in his dealings with the pirates, brought him into prominent notice. The son of a poor Ayrshire cottager, he had worked himself up, from before the mast, to the command of a ship. Soon after his return to England, the directors appointed him to be their supervisor on the west coast of Sumatra, and, before he sailed, a provisional commission was given him to succeed to the Presidentship of Madras, on a vacancy occurring. Eighteen months later, he took his seat as governor at Fort St. George. His six years of office were distinguished by his efforts to put an end to many abuses that had grown up in the Company's affairs. He left India with a fortune of £100,000, made by private trade, and settled down near his birthplace, which he had not revisited since he left it as a boy. He died in 1746.

Note.—The account of England's cruise in the *Cassandra*, given in Johnson's *History of the Pirates*, is evidently taken from Lazenby's narrative to the E.I.C. Directors. Macrae's account of the capture of the *Cassandra*, given by Johnson, appears also to have been part of a similar report to the directors, but the report itself has disappeared. Additional information is to be found in the logs of the *Greenwich* and *London*.

CHAPTER 8

Expedition Against Colaba

As long as their forces had been occupied with the French war and the Highland rising, the English ministry had been powerless to check the depredations of the pirates, which had become intolerable both in the East and West Indies. Now Europe was at peace, and measures could be concerted to put a stop to the evil. As usual, the Peace of Utrecht was followed by an increase of piracy, through the privateersmen being thrown out of employment.

On the 5th September, 1717, a royal proclamation was published, offering a free pardon, to all pirates on the American coast surrendering within one year, for all piracies committed before the 5th January. As rewards for the capture of pirate ships, to every captain £100, to other officers £40, to petty officers £30, and to ordinary seamen £20 were to be paid on conviction of the offenders. To pirates, a reward of £200 was offered for the surrender of a pirate captain or commander before the 6th September, 1718. The effect of the proclamation, in conjunction with the measures taken in the Bahamas, was very great. By the 1st July, 1719, to which date the time of grace was extended, all but three or four of the most desperate rovers had retired from business. But against the most audacious of them more vigorous measures were necessary.

It was of little use to hunt down pirates at sea, so long as their haunts in the Bahamas and Madagascar were allowed to flourish, and, as the West Indian rovers were the most mischievous to European trade, the Bahamas were first taken in hand.

During the war, the Bahamas had been twice taken and plundered by the French and Spanish; all semblance of authority had disappeared, and it was estimated that there were upwards of two thousand pirates in and about Providence. In 1718, Captain Woodes Rogers leased the islands for twenty-one years, from the proprietors, and received a commission as governor; he sailed, for Providence, with a naval force and powers to offer an amnesty to all who submitted. Five or six well-known pirate captains made their peace with the government, and a number of their crews, though some of them went back to their old trade before long. England, La Buze, and others slipped away and made for Madagascar. A council was then formed, consisting of six of the adventurers and six of the inhabitants who had never been pirates themselves. This was followed by the submission of others; some were hung, and order of a sort was re-established in the Bahamas.

The coasts of Virginia and North Carolina were at this time beset by a number of pirates, the most notorious of whom was Edward Teach, *alias* Blackbeard, a Bristol man, who had begun his piratical career in the spring of 1717; the most sinister figure in the annals of piracy. Pirate captains were, as a rule, chosen by their crews, and if their conduct was unsatisfactory to the rovers, they were deposed and sometimes put to death or marooned; but Teach, as fearless as he was merciless, ruled his crew by terror. As an instance of his savage humour, it is related that on one occasion, in a drinking bout, he blew out the light and fired two pistols among his companions, wounding Israel Hands, his sailing master, severely.

On being asked why he did it, he damned them, and said if he did not kill one of them now and then, they would forget who he was. So impressed were his crew with his wickedness, that they believed they carried the devil on board, who appeared at intervals among them as one of the crew, but could not be identified as belonging to the ship's company. Once he fought the *Scarborough*, a man-of-war of thirty guns, and beat her off. He boldly went ashore when he pleased, forcing the governor of North Carolina to marry him, and to supply him with medicines for his crew. With his face covered with black hair, and a beard of extravagant length, fantastically tied up in ribbons, he presented a wild and truculent figure that was the terror of the coast.

An extract of a journal he kept, found after his death, is given by Johnson—

> Such a day, rum all out:—Our company somewhat sober: A damned confusion amongst us!—Rogues a plotting;—great talk of separation.—So I looked sharp for a prize;—such a day took one, with a great deal of liquor on board, so kept the Company hot, damned hot, then all things went well again.

Eden, the governor of North Carolina, was suspected of sharing in Teach's plunder, and his conduct was so suspicious that it could only be set down to dishonesty or to extreme pusillanimity; so, in their distress, the North Carolina planters sought the assistance of the Governor of Virginia. There were at this time two men-of-war, the *Pearl* and the *Lime*, lying in the James river, but their size was too great to permit of their searching the creeks and inlets frequented by Teach; therefore, two small sloops, without guns, were fitted out and placed under command of Maynard, first lieutenant of the *Pearl*. At the same time a proclamation was published in Virginia offering rewards for the apprehension of pirates, with a special reward of £100 for Teach. Though the whole had been planned with great secrecy, Teach received warnings from friends on shore, but paid no attention to them, and Maynard surprised him at anchor in a small inlet.

Teach cut his cable and tried to stand out to sea, but ran aground. Maynard anchored within half gunshot and set to work to lighten his sloops, while Teach roared out curses and threats, to which Maynard replied that he expected no quarter and would give none. Just as Maynard was ready to attack, Teach got afloat and bore down on the sloops, giving them a broadside that partially disabled one sloop, and killed or wounded twenty men in Maynard's. Nothing discouraged, Maynard kept his men under cover and ran the pirate aboard, and was at once attacked by Teach with fourteen men.

Teach and Maynard met hand to hand, and there was a desperate encounter, Teach fighting like a ferocious animal at bay. Maynard's sword broke, but he was saved by one of his men coming to his assistance, and Teach at last fell dead on the deck of the sloop with twenty-five wounds. The second sloop, meanwhile, had boarded and captured the pirate ship, and Maynard sailed back to the James River with Teach's head at his bowsprit. Fifteen of the pirates were taken alive, of whom thirteen were hung.

A year after Teach's death there appeared on the American coast Bartholomew Roberts, a Welshman from Haverford west, who, for over two years, was the scourge of the American and African traders. It was said of him that he was a sober man who drank tea constantly, which made him an object of suspicion to his crew. His temperance did not prevent him from being the most wantonly wicked pirate who sailed the seas. In a Newfoundland harbour, on one occasion, he burned and sank twenty-one vessels, destroyed the fisheries and stages, and wrought all the havoc he could, out of pure wantonness.

On another occasion, he captured a slaver with eighty slaves on board, and burned it, slaves and all, because it would cost too much time and trouble to unshackle the unfortunate wretches.

At the same time, he was a man of order and method. He drew up a set of rules, to which his crew subscribed, in which, among other things, it was laid down that no women should be allowed on board; dice and gambling were prohibited; lights were put out at 8 o'clock; and musicians were exempt from playing on Sundays. The chaplain of Cape Coast Castle having been captured, he was pressed to join the pirates, being promised that nothing would be required of him except to make punch and say prayers. On his declining the office, all church property was restored to him "except three prayer books and a bottle-screw."

In pursuit of Roberts, the British government despatched Captain Challoner Ogle, with the *Swallow* and *Weymouth*. Failing to find him in American waters, Ogle steered for the African shore, and, on the 5th February, 1722, when separated from the *Weymouth*, he came on the pirates at anchor off Cape Lopez. Putting the *Swallow* about, and handling his sails as if in confusion and alarm, Ogle stood out to sea, pursued by the *Ranger*. When well out of sight of land, the *Ranger* was allowed to draw up, and the pirate crew suddenly found themselves under the fire of a sixty-gun ship, for which their own thirty-two guns were no match, and after a short engagement the black flag was hauled down.

On the 10th, Ogle stood in again to engage the *Royal Fortune*, disposing his flags to make the pirates believe his ship had been captured by the *Ranger*. Roberts fought with desperation when he discovered the ruse. Dressed in rich crimson damask, a scarlet feather in his hat, a gold chain with large diamond cross round his neck, he made a resistance worthy of his reputation, determined to blow up his ship rather than yield. At the main he hoisted a black flag, on which were displayed a skeleton and a man with a flaming sword; the jack was black, showing a man standing on two skulls, and St. George's ensign was at the ensign staff. After a desperate encounter, Roberts was slain by a grape-shot, and the *Royal Fortune* carried by boarding, the pirates resisting to the last. Out of two hundred and seventy-six men captured in the two ships, fifty-two were executed, all of them Englishmen. Ogle was knighted for his able and gallant conduct.

The re-establishment of authority at the Bahamas had led to an increase in the numbers of the Madagascar pirates; so Commodore

Thomas Matthews was despatched to the East Indies with a strong squadron, consisting of the *Lyon*, 50 guns; *Salisbury*, 40 guns; *Exeter*, 50 guns; and *Shoreham*, 20 guns. The Company's ship *Grantham* was also placed under his orders, to act as a store-ship. In Byng's successful action with the Spanish, off Cape Passaro (August, 1718), Matthews had commanded the *Kent* with credit; but with the exception of courage, he apparently failed to possess a single quality for independent command. Irascible, domineering to his subordinates, and insolent to all others he was brought in contact with, he was entirely devoid of judgment or discretion. Twenty years later, when he became better known, Walpole wrote of his 'brutal manners,' and Horace Mann nicknamed him 'Il Furibondo.' There could not have been a worse selection for the work in hand.

The desire of the directors was that the squadron should, before going to Bombay, proceed to St. Augustine's Bay and St. Mary's. Thence, that a ship should be detached to Bourbon, where it was supposed a new pirate settlement was being formed; after which, they wished the squadron to proceed to the mouth of the Red Sea, where pirates would in all probability be found waiting for the Indian ships in July and August. But Matthews had views of his own, and was not much concerned with the wishes of the directors, who had designs of opening up trade with Madagascar, and, as a preliminary step, desired to see the pirate settlements rooted out.

In February, 1721, the squadron sailed from Spithead, with orders to rendezvous at St. Augustine's Bay. Soon after leaving the Channel, the *Salisbury* and *Exeter* were dismasted in a storm, and were obliged to put into Lisbon to repair damages. Matthews continued his voyage with the *Lyon* and the *Shoreham* to St. Augustine's Bay. He found no pirate ships there at the time, and good policy demanded that he should await the *Salisbury* and the *Exeter*. Instead of doing so, he continued his voyage to Bombay, where he arrived on the 27th September. Before leaving, he entrusted to the natives of St. Augustine's Bay a letter for Captain Cockburn, of the *Salisbury*, in which a number of particulars were given of the squadron.

The proceeding was so ill-advised and so well calculated to defeat the object of the squadron's coming into Indian waters, that it was believed in the squadron that Matthews had done it purposely to put the pirates on their guard. Whether this was his intention or not, it serves to show the opinion held of him by those under his command. Soon after Matthews' departure, Taylor and La Buze reached St. Augustine's

Bay, read the letter, and sailed at once for Fort Dauphin, in the south-eastern end of Madagascar.

The *Salisbury* and *Exeter* arrived soon afterwards, and getting no news either of Matthews or the pirates, sailed for Bombay. These proceedings were not of happy augury for the success of the expedition. The pirates had information of the squadron being in the Indian seas, and were doubtless kept henceforth informed, from time to time, of its movements through their various sources of intelligence. Taylor, satisfied with his gains, sailed for the West Indies and surrendered to the Spaniards, who gave him a commission.

Matthews' first act on dropping anchor, was to force the native vessels in harbour, belonging to Bombay traders, to strike the English colours they were in the habit of displaying, and he next embarked in a squabble with the governor as to who was to fire the first salute, a matter that was not settled without many messages to and fro. The officers of the squadron, taking their cue from Matthews, 'looked as much superior to us,' Downing tells us, 'as the greatness of their ambition could possibly lead them. There were daily duels fought by one or other of them, and challenges perpetually sent round the island by the gentlemen of the navy.' The duels seem mostly to have taken place among the naval officers, who must have been a quarrelsome lot.

On the voyage from England, Mr. Mitchell and Mr. Sutherland, 'son of My Lord Sutherland,' had quarrelled, and Mitchell, considering himself aggrieved, demanded his discharge on arrival at Bombay, which was granted. He then sent a challenge to Sutherland, who wounded and disabled him. But all duels were not so harmless. A few days afterwards, Sutherland and Dalrymple, 'grandson of Sir David Dalrymple, His Majesty's Advocate for Scotland,' both midshipmen, quarrelled over dice, and fought a duel, without seconds, the following morning; when Dalrymple was run through the body and killed on the spot—a fate that was apparently not altogether undeserved. Sutherland was tried by court-martial, found guilty of murder, and sentenced to death; but as it was necessary for the death-warrant to be signed by the king, it was arranged to carry him a prisoner to England.

Touching at Barbadoes, he made his escape, and remained there till a free pardon was granted him. Not long afterwards a duel, arising out of a quarrel about a lady's health, was fought between Stepney, the second lieutenant, and Berkeley, the third lieutenant of the *Salisbury*, in which both were badly wounded. Stepney died a fortnight after the duel, but, as the surgeon certified that he had not died of his wound, Berkeley was not brought to a court-martial.

Meanwhile, great preparations were being made for a fresh campaign against Angria, and while these bickerings went on among the subordinates, the governor and Matthews were engaged in planning the attack. Long before Matthews' arrival, negotiations had been opened between the Portuguese Viceroy, Francisco José de Sampaio e Castro, and the Bombay Council, for a joint attack on Colaba. Through the management of Mr. Robert Cowan, who had been deputed, in March, to Goa, for the purpose, a treaty of mutual co-operation had been drawn up, by which the Bombay Council undertook to furnish two thousand men and five ships. The Portuguese authorities undertook to furnish an equal force.

The negotiation was not completed till the beginning of September, and Cowan, in recognition of the ability he had displayed, was given a seat in the council. The combined forces were to assemble at Chaul, then a Portuguese possession, and march overland to attack Colaba. Forgetting the old adage about selling the skin of the bear while the animal was still alive, it was further agreed that Colaba, after capture, was to be the property of Portugal, while Gheriah was to be handed over to the English. The arrival of Matthews' squadron therefore brought a welcome addition to the Bombay armaments.

A camp was formed for the expeditionary force; drilling was the order of the day; Cowan was named general, and various commissions as colonels, majors, and captains were granted to officers of the navy who volunteered for land service. On the 30th October, a seven days' fast was ordered, to secure the Divine blessing on the undertaking, and the chaplain was directed to preach an appropriate sermon.

On the 29th November, the expedition left Bombay, and anchored off Chaul, where the Portuguese force had already assembled. The English force consisted of 655 Europeans and *topasses*, a troop of 40 horsemen, and 1514 *sepoys*. Matthews also contributed 200 seamen, of whom 50 were to serve the guns. The artillery consisted of two 24-pounders, two 18-pounders, four 9-pounders, six small field guns, two mortars, and eight coehorns. The Portuguese force consisted of 1000 Europeans, 160 horsemen, 350 volunteers, and 2400 *sepoys*, with six 24-pounders, six 18-pounders, ten field pieces, and eight mortars, commanded by the General of the North. The viceroy was also present. Such a force, combined with the men-of-war, was sufficient, under proper direction, to have destroyed all Angria's strongholds along the coast.

Some delay was caused by the necessity of building a bridge over the Ragocim River, and then the army advanced, to be quickly brought to a standstill again till sufficient transport could be brought from Bombay. On the 12th December, after marching round the head of the Alibagh River, the army encamped close to Alibagh fort; while the men-of-war anchored in the roads. During the march, a few of Angria's horsemen had been seen from time to time. On one occasion, while the viceroy, accompanied by Matthews, Cowan, and other commanders, was riding to view the country, a horseman approached them under cover of a cactus hedge, and threw his lance, wounding Matthews in the thigh. Matthews vainly pursued him, beside himself with rage at his wound and at his pistols missing fire.

On the 13th, an assault was made on the fort, though the heavy guns had not been landed. Outside the fort there were fifteen hundred horse and a thousand foot sent by Sahoojee to Angria's assistance. The Portuguese were to face them, while five hundred English soldiers and marines, led by naval officers, were to force the gateway and scale the rampart. Common sense demanded that Sahoojee's force outside the fort should be disposed of, and the heavy guns that had been brought with so much labour from Chaul should be mounted and used, before any attempt at an assault was projected; but there was a woeful absence of ordinary capacity among the commanders. At four in the afternoon, the little force under Brathwaite, first lieutenant of the *Lyon*, who held the rank of colonel for the occasion, advanced to the assault.

The gateway was blocked, and could not be forced; many of the scaling ladders were too short, and the affair resolved itself into a struggle, by a small number who had gained the rampart, to maintain themselves, while the rest remained exposed to the fire from the walls. In the midst of it, Sahoojee's force advanced on the Portuguese, who broke and fled in wild confusion, leaving the English, force to their fate. The assaulting party, seeing their danger, drew off, leaving many of their wounded behind them, the whole force gave ground, and soon there was a wild rush for the camp, luckily not followed by the Mahratta horsemen.

Thirty-three had been killed and twenty-seven wounded; among the latter, Lieutenant Bellamy of the navy, who had behaved with great dash and bravery. Matthews' marines suffered heavily. Though wanting in discipline, they displayed much courage. All the field guns and a great deal of ammunition fell into the hands of the Mahrattas.

The whole blame was laid on the Portuguese, to whom treachery was imputed. Matthews, always violent, flew at the General of the North and assaulted him,[1] and treated the viceroy not much better. A little more enterprise on the part of the Mahrattas would have destroyed the whole force. The following day some heavy guns were landed, and a four-gun battery was constructed. But the Portuguese had had enough of it, and were determined to withdraw.

From the beginning, there had been little cordiality between the ill-matched allies. In the English camp, Cowan was devoid of military experience or instinct, and commanded little confidence among men habituated to defeat in their attacks on Angrian strongholds; while Matthews, violent and overbearing, claimed a right to direct operations that he knew nothing about. The Portuguese, on their side, proud in the recollection of the great position they had once held on the Malabar coast, and which, though now fast falling into decay, was still immeasurably superior to that of the English merchants, were disgusted at the constant drunkenness, quarrelling, and want of discipline among the English, and incensed at the charge of treachery, for which there was no justification.

Feigning illness, the viceroy betook himself to his ship. Angria saw his opportunity of breaking up the alliance, and opened negotiations with him. On the 17th, the viceroy wrote to the English, proposing a suspension of arms. With a bad grace they were obliged to consent, seeing in the negotiation, which was against the compact that neither should treat separately, farther confirmation of their suspicion of treachery. Angria granted the Portuguese full reparation for injuries, and formed an offensive and defensive alliance with them. The English were left to shift for themselves. Full of wrath, they embarked at once, and sailed for Bombay on the 28th.

While the force was engaged at Colaba, the Malwans[2] strove to make a diversion in Angria's favour by attacking English ships, under pretence that they were Portuguese vessels; they being at war with Goa at the time. The Sunda Rajah also attacked a private English ship, but was beaten off. In the Gulf, the Bombay sloop *Prince* took a Muscat ship of fourteen guns, but after some days was obliged to relinquish its prize to a Muscat squadron.

It is impossible not to sympathize with Boone's disappointment

---

1. 'Thrust his cane in his mouth.'—*Downing*.
2. Malwan was a small fortified harbour belonging to Kolapore, about sixty miles north of Goa. The Malwans were noted pirates.

at the failure of this long-planned expedition, which he had looked forward to as the crowning achievement of his presidency. The time had come for him to return to England. His successor, Mr. William. Phipps, had arrived from Mocha, in August, and had taken the second seat in Council, while awaiting Boone's departure. Boone's last year in Bombay was embittered by a dangerous intrigue against him, headed by Parker and Braddyll, two of the Council. Investigation showed that they had plotted to seize his person, and had even uttered threats against his life. Being arrested and ordered to leave Bombay, they fled to Goa.

After a time, Braddyll made his way in a small boat to Bombay, and sought protection on board the *Lyon*, which was readily extended to him by Matthews. As Braddyll's name appears among those present in Council in Bombay, in 1723, he must have succeeded in making his peace with the Company. Under the Company's rule, in those days, all but the worst offences were condoned, so long as they were not directly aimed at the Company's trade. A plot against the governor's freedom might be pardoned, but, for assistance given to the Ostenders there was no *locus poenitentiae*.

On the 9th January, Boone embarked on board the *London*, after making over the governorship to Mr. Phipps, followed by the good wishes of the community. During his six years of office he had proved himself a faithful and zealous servant of the Company: 'a gentleman of as much honour and good sense as any that ever sat in that chair,' according to Hamilton. He had found Bombay with a languishing trade and open to attack. Under his fostering care, trade had improved, so that merchants from Bengal and Madras had found it profitable to settle there. A good wall had been built to guard the town against sudden raids, and a respectable naval force had been created to keep piracy in check. He deserves remembrance as the first Bombay governor who tried to put down the coast pirates by active measures.

Though his expeditions against them had been uniformly unsuccessful, he had taught Angria that the Company's trade could not be attacked with impunity, and his ill-success was entirely due to the worthlessness of his instruments. At his departure, salutes were fired from every gun ashore and afloat, except from Matthews' squadron, which did not fire a gun. As he sailed down the coast, accompanied by the *Victoria* and *Revenge*, loaded with stores for Carwar and Anjengo, he was attacked by Angria's squadron, but beat them off. Off Anjediva he came on the Kempsant's *grabs* plundering a ship, which he rescued.

One of the *grabs* was taken and another driven ashore; and so he was gratified with a small success over his inveterate enemies, as he bid farewell to the Indian coast.

As soon as Matthews had returned to Bombay, after the Alibagh fiasco, he applied himself to what, to him, was the principal reason for his coming to India, *viz.* private trade. For the Company's interests he did not care a button; in fact, anything that injured the Company found an advocate in him. As for the pirates, if they did not come in his way, he was not going to trouble himself much about them. To enrich himself by starting a private trade of his own, was his one object, and, with this end in view, he sailed for Surat. With him he took Mrs. Braddyll and Mrs. Wyche, with sundry chests of treasure, in spite of Phipps' remonstrances: the estates of both having been attached by the council.

In Surat he tried to raise a large sum for a venture in the China trade; but the arbitrary conduct of the king's officers had raised so much distrust among the native merchants, that he was unsuccessful. Within three weeks he was back again in Bombay, and was at once involved in an angry correspondence with the council. Not confining himself to an acrimonious exchange of letters, he affixed at the sea gate an insulting proclamation. Phipps ordered it to be removed, on which Matthews wrote that, if it were not at once replaced, he would publish it by beat of drum through Bombay, and, should any resistance be offered, he would not leave a house standing in the place. In this dilemma the council consented to replace it, but, to save their dignity, added a notice that it was licensed by the secretary. It is difficult to see how this improved the matter. However, Matthews sailed the next day for Madagascar, so no doubt the proclamation did not long remain after his departure.

His absence from Bombay, though doubtless felt as a relief by Phipps and the council, was probably, before long, a cause of regret in the troubles that shortly beset them: but for the moment we will follow his movements. Not contented with his quarrels with the council, Matthews was soon at daggers drawn with his own captains. First he proposed to them to employ their ships in trading, on condition that two-thirds of the profits were to be his. The captains refused to have anything to do with the proposal. He had already had a quarrel with Cockburn, his second in command, the first of many that were to follow. Before leaving Bombay, a quarrel arose between him and Sir Robert Johnson, of the *Exeter*. Johnson threw up his command, and took passage for England in one of the Company's ships, which was lost with all hands on the voyage.

With Sir Robert Johnson, his son, a lieutenant in the navy, perished. Brathwaite was appointed to the command of the *Exeter*. It had already come to be widely known that anybody who was in trouble with the Company would find countenance and protection from Matthews. He told the Portuguese officials that the Company's vessels were only traders, and therefore not entitled to a salute, gun for gun. This matter of salutes was a very important one in Matthews' eyes. Every trading ship, however small it might be, carried guns, and there was a great deal of saluting. In acknowledging such salutes Matthews always responded with three or four less guns than were given him. On one occasion there is a record of his replying with one gun only.[3] Wherever Matthews could find an opportunity for lowering the credit or hurting the interests of the Company, he seized it.

On reaching Carpenter's Bay in Mauritius, he found an impudent message from the pirates, 'writ on Captain Carpenter's tomb with a piece of charcoal,' to the effect that they had been expecting him and had gone to Port Dauphin. The squadron next proceeded to Bourbon, where they sold some casks of *arrack* and *madeira* to the French for a very good profit, and thence proceeded to Charnock Point, St. Mary's Island, Madagascar. Here they found the wrecks of several merchant ships that had been run ashore by the pirates. Scattered on the beach were lying their cargoes, china ware, rich drugs and spices, cloth, guns, and other articles, lying where the pirates had cast them. Men waded knee-deep in pepper, cloves, and cinnamon, such was the quantity.

In shallow water were lying the remains of a fine Jeddah ship that had been taken, with thirteen *lakhs* of treasure on board, by a pirate named Conden, who commanded a ship called the *Flying Dragon*. Matthews at once began to transfer the guns and such commodities as were least damaged to his own ships. A flag of truce had been first sent ashore to communicate with England and the other pirates, but it was found that they had fled inland. A week later, a white man, accompanied by a well-armed guard of natives, made his appearance. He told them that he was a Jamaica man named John Plantain, that he had been a pirate, but was tired of the trade, and had settled down on the spot.

This John Plantain was a man of some note in the piratical world. Every and England had sailed with him, and treated him with much

---
3. When Watson came to India, he returned salutes gun for gun.

consideration and some fear. He had made himself master of a considerable tract of country, so that the pirates had given him the name of the King of Ranter Bay.[4] He gave an invitation to Matthews to visit his castle, where he entertained some of the officers of the squadron. Matthews' first idea was to seize him, but finding that John Plantain had a good number of armed natives with him, besides a Scotchman and a Dane, and that his castle had plenty of guns mounted, he decided to trade with him instead. The pirates made no secret of having taken part in the capture of the Goa viceroy's ship, and of a rich native vessel with eighteen *lakhs* of *rupees* on board.

So hats, shoes, stockings, wine, and *arrack* were made over to John Plantain, for which he paid a good price in gold and diamonds. In spite of his notions as to piracy, John Plantain showed himself an honester man than Matthews. Having paid liberally for the things he had bought, he left the hogsheads of wine and arrack on the beach under a small guard. As soon as his back was turned, Matthews manned his boats, brought off all the liquor he had been paid for, and some of the native guard as well. After which notable achievement he sailed away for Bengal, consoling himself with the thought that he was not like one of "those vile pirates, who, after committing many evil actions, had settled down among a parcel of heathens to indulge themselves in all sorts of vice."[5]

After a fortnight at Charnock's Point, the squadron made its way round the north of Madagascar to Manigaro (Manankara) Bay, whence they steered for Johanna. As the directors afterwards remarked, Matthews ought to have divided his squadron, and searched both coasts of the great island; but his heart was not in the quest for pirates; he was bent only on trade. Sending the *Salisbury* and *Exeter* to cruise towards Socotra, he took the *Lyon* and *Shoreham* to Bengal, and, in the beginning of August, he was at anchor in the Hoogly, near Diamond Harbour. There he remained till the end of October. There were no pirates in the Bay of Bengal, but the sugar trade was very lucrative, and he wanted to invest in it.

He was not long in Calcutta without coming to loggerheads with the council concerning Mrs. Gyfford, who, as Mrs. Chown, has al-

---

4. Perhaps Autongil Bay.

5. This account of Matthews' visit to Madagascar rests to a great extent on the narrative of Clement Downing, who held the rating of a midshipman on board the *Salisbury* at the time. It is confirmed by the logs of the *Lyon* and *Salisbury*. He makes no attempt to conceal his opinion of Matthews' misdoings. He also gives the history of John Plantain, who finally made his way to Gheriah, and took service with Angria.

ready been mentioned in these pages,[6] and whose third husband had perished in the Anjengo massacre eighteen months before. In flying from Anjengo she had carried off the factory books, together with all the money she could lay her hands on. As the Company had large claims on Gyfford's estate, the council was bent on making her disgorge. Matthews espoused her quarrel, as he did that of all who were in the Company's bad books, and, in defiance of the council, carried her off to Bombay, and eventually to England.

---

6. See chapter 4.

Chapter 9

A Troubled Year in Bombay

The year succeeding Boone's departure was a stirring one in Bombay. On the 27th February, the *Eagle* and *Hunter* galleys, while off Bassein, convoying a Surat ship, were attacked by four of Angria's grabs. After a five-hours' engagement, during which the *Hunter* made three attempts at boarding, an unlucky shot ignited some loose powder, and the galley blew up, every soul on board perishing.

A similar explosion, though less serious, took place on board the *Eagle*, which forced her to take refuge in a shattered condition in Saragon harbour. Here the Portuguese showed such unfriendliness, that the Council were obliged to send other galleys to protect and bring the *Eagle* away.

Since the conclusion of the Portuguese treaty with Angria, an angry correspondence had gone on between Goa and Bombay, and soon the old causes of quarrel were revived. The chief of these was the levying of duties at certain places. The General of the North, who had tried to force on a quarrel a year before, smarting, doubtless, under the treatment he had received from Matthews at the siege of Alibagh, began to levy duties on provisions coming from Bombay to Portuguese territory. Phipps retaliated by levying customs duties at Mahim, which the Portuguese had always claimed to be free to both nations. The quarrel grew hot. The General of the North forbade all communication with Bombay, and, on the 26th May, a British *gallivat* was fired on at Mahim.

The council resolved to uphold their rights, but were in a poor condition to do so. Meanwhile, it became known that Angria's assistance was being invited by the Portuguese. On the 23rd June, a party from Bombay landed and destroyed the Portuguese fort at Corlem, and shelled Bandara. Captain Loader, of the *Revenge*, without orders, burned the undefended village on Elephanta, for which he was suspended from his command; but at the end of a week he was reinstated. Want of shipping for a time prevented any vigorous prosecution of hostilities on the part of the council. They were obliged to remain on the defensive, while Portuguese galleys cruised off the island, making occasional raids, killing a militiaman or two, and burning villages. Mahim, Riva, and Darvi were all raided, but with small benefit to the assailants. On the 28th August, at night, a Portuguese force landed and destroyed the fort at Warlee, assisted by the treachery of a renegade Portuguese. On the 3rd and 4th September, two attempts to land at the Breach were repulsed, and the council were cheered by the arrival of the *Salisbury* and *Exeter* from their Red Sea cruise.

Cockburn, of the *Salisbury*, less churlish than Matthews, at once put two pinnaces and seventy-six men at the council's disposal. A small expedition of eleven *gallivats* under Stanton was also fitted out, and a battery erected by the Portuguese at Surey to hinder provisions coming into Bombay, was captured. One man of the *Exeter* was killed and another wounded. Just then came news that Angria was fitting out an expedition of five thousand men to attack Carwar, and the *Exeter* sailed there to defend the factory.

At the beginning of November, the tide turned. News having been received that some of Angria's *grabs* were cruising off Warlee, the *Victoria* and *Revenge*, manned with crews from the *Salisbury*, were sent out. After a hot engagement, Angria's commodore, a Dutchman, was killed, and his ship, mounting sixteen guns, taken.

On the same day that the captured ship was brought into Bombay, two other captures entered the harbour. The directors had sent out from England three galleys, the *Bombay*, the *Bengal*, and the *Fort St. George*, manned with sailors from the Thames. As they were proceeding up the coast they found themselves dogged for two days by two strange *grabs* showing no colours. Resolved to put an end to it, on the third day, on the 1st November, off Cape Ramus, they shortened sail and called on the strangers to show their colours. They proved to be Portuguese, and the English hails were answered by threats and shouts of defiance. The *Bengal* then fired a shot across the bows of the leading *grab*, which was answered by a broadside, killing the second mate and two seamen.

The *Bombay* closed in, while the *Fort St. George* turned its attention to the second *grab*. In half an hour both of the Portuguese vessels struck their colours, and the galleys continued their course for Bombay with their two prizes, each carrying twenty guns. Such was the difference made by having British seamen, instead of the miserable crews that had hitherto manned the Company's ships.

It was well for the Bombay Council that Matthews had been absent while this was going on. For two months and a half he had remained at anchor in the Hooghly. Early in December he reached Bombay, and at once recommenced his quarrels with the council and his captains. Cockburn, of the *Salisbury*, was placed under arrest, presumably for the assistance he had given to the council. After a time he was transferred to the *Exeter*, and ordered to proceed to England.

In coming up the coast Matthews had touched at Goa, and informed the viceroy of his disapproval of the Company's actions, and that his squadron would soon be leaving the Indian seas. But the viceroy had had enough fighting. The capture of his *grabs* had brought him to reason. He laid all the blame for recent hostilities on the General of the North, and a peaceful accommodation was come to with the council, Matthews being disregarded.

In spite of Matthews' failure to destroy the Madagascar pirates, the presence of his squadron in Indian waters impelled them to seek safety in the West Indies, and henceforward they ceased to be dangerous to the trade-ships of India. The Madagascar settlements lingered on till they died a natural death. Angria, too, had been tamed by the slaying of his commodore and the capture of his ships. For years the seaborne trade of Bombay had not been so little subject to molestation as it was for the next three or four years.

Matthews had sent home two of his ships, remaining, himself, to do another year's trading, during which he lost no opportunity of worrying and insulting the Company's officers. Everybody at variance with the council found an advocate in him. A Parsee broker, named Bomanjee, was under arrest for fraud; Matthews demanded his surrender. The council placed Bomanjee in close confinement in the fort, to prevent his being carried off. Matthews promised Bomanjee's sons he would take one of them to England, and undertook to make the directors see things in a proper light.

Men charged with abominable crimes received countenance from him. He told the Council that they were only traders, and had no power to punish anybody. The crown alone had power to punish. He (Matthews) represented the crown, and was answerable only to the King of England. One may picture to one's self the satisfaction with which, at the end of the year, the council learned that Matthews was really going.

In December, 1723, he set sail for England. During the two years he had been in the Indian seas he had accomplished nothing he ought to have done, and done almost everything he ought not to have done. He had been sent out to suppress the pirates and to protect the Company's interests. He had not captured a single pirate ship or rooted out a single pirate haunt. Claiming, as a King's officer, to be exempt from the provisions of the Company's charter, he had indulged in private trade, and had even had dealings with the pirates. He had flouted the Company's authority wherever it existed, and had encouraged others to resist it.

Every person who had a dispute with the Company received protection from him. He told the Goa authorities that the Company's vessels were only traders, and therefore not entitled to the salutes they had always received. He had refused to give up the Company's sailors whom he encouraged to desert to his ship. He forbade the Bombay traders to fly British colours, but allowed his own trading friends to do so. He had gone trading to Bengal and Mocha, where there were no pirates; two months and a half he had spent in the Hooghly; three months and a half he had spent at Madras and St. David's for trade purposes; and, when the quarrel between the Bombay authorities and the Portuguese was going on, he gave out that he would send the Goa viceroy a petticoat, as an old woman, if he did not take every one of the Company's ships. He had quarrelled with all his captains, and one of them, Sir Robert Johnson, owed his death to him.

At Surat he had found a discharged servant of the Company, one Mr. Wyche, on whose departure the governor had laid an embargo till his accounts were cleared. Matthews took him and his eleven chests of treasure on board his ship, in defiance of the governor's orders, and put him ashore at Calicut, whence he escaped to French territory. From Surat also he carried to England the broker's son, Rustumjee Nowrojee, to worry the Directors. He carried off Mrs. Gyfford, and brought her to England in his ship. His last act on the coast was to call at Anjengo, in order to obtain property she claimed there: but it is probable that he also secured a cargo of pepper.

It is small wonder that, on his arrival in England, in July, 1724, the wrath of the directors was kindled against him, and an account of his misbehaviour was forwarded to the Secretary of State. The naval authorities called on the directors to produce their witnesses for the charge of trading with the pirates. The difficulty of doing so was obvious, as the witnesses were all under Matthews' command; so the charge was dropped, and the directors sued him in the Court of Exchequer for infringing their charter by private trading.

Meanwhile the naval authorities had their own account to settle with Matthews; Captain Maine, of the *Shoreham*, having made various charges against him. In the last week of December, 1724, he was brought to a court-martial on board the *Sandwich* in the Medway, and the finding of the court was thus recorded:—

> The court, having read the complaints of the directors of the E.I. Co. of several irregularities said to be committed by Captain Thomas Matthews while commander-in-chief of a squadron of His Majesty's ships sent to the East Indies, a publication being made three several times, if any person or persons were attending on behalf of the said directors, in order to prove the several matters therein contained, and not any appearing, the court proceeded on the complaints exhibited by Captain Covil Maine, and having strictly examined into the several particulars and matters therein contained and heard divers witnesses upon oath, they are unanimously of opinion, that the said Captain Matthews hath in all respects complied with his instructions, except that of receiving merchandize on board before the late Act of Parliament, instituted an act for the more effectual suppression of piracy, came to hand, but not afterwards; and it appearing to the court, that he had sent men irregularly to merchant ships, and finding he falls under the 33rd Article of War, they have resolved he be mulcted four months' pay, and that the same be applied for the benefit of the chest of Chatham, and he is hereby mulcted accordingly.

Six weeks later, the directors obtained a decree against him in the Court of Exchequer, for £13,676 17*s*. 6*d*., which, according to Act of Parliament, was doubled as a penalty.

In 1742, Matthews again found favour with an English Ministry. He was appointed minister at Turin and commander-in-chief in the Mediterranean.

In February, 1744, he encountered a combined French and Spanish fleet off Toulon. His behaviour to his subordinates had excited their ill-will to such an extent that his second in command and many of the captains refused to follow him. The allied fleet escaped with the loss of one ship only.

Both admirals and five captains were cashiered, and that is the last we hear of Matthews. The remembrance of his behaviour long rankled in the minds of the directors, and twenty years elapsed before they could again bring themselves to apply for the despatch of a royal squadron to the Indian seas.[1]

---

[1] The squadron under Barnet, which was sent out in 1744, on the declaration of war with France.

Chapter 10

Twenty-Six Years of Conflict

As an instance of the miseries to which men were exposed by Angria's piracies, may be mentioned the case of Mr. Curgenven, a private merchant of Madras. Being bound on a trading voyage to China, he sailed from Surat in August, 1720, in the *Charlotte*. Before he could get clear of the coast, he was captured by Angria's fleet and carried into Gheriah. There he remained for nearly ten years, during the whole of which time he was made to wear fetters and work as a slave. In spite of the letters he was able to send to Bombay, nothing appears to have been done to procure his liberty. At last, on payment of a ransom, he was set free, and joined his wife in England. But the fetters he had worn so long had injured one of his legs, and amputation was necessary. As he was recovering from the operation, an artery burst, and he died on the spot.

With Boone's departure from India the attacks on the Angrian strongholds came to an end. They were henceforth regarded as impregnable, and Boone's successors contented themselves with checking the Angrian power at sea.

In June, 1729, Conajee Angria died. He left two legitimate sons, Sakhajee and Sumbhajee; three illegitimate sons, Toolajee, Mannajee, and Yessajee. Sakhajee established himself at Colaba, while Sumbhajee Angria remained at Severndroog, to carry on the predatory policy of their father. In March, 1734, Sakhajee died, and Mannajee and Yessajee were sent to hold Colaba for Sumbhajee. Before long, Mannajee quarrelled with Sumbhajee and Yessajee, and fled to Chaul. The Portuguese espoused his quarrel, and furnished him with a force against Colaba, which was taken; Mannajee gallantly leading the assault, sword in hand. He at once imprisoned Yessajee, and put out his eyes.

As soon as the Portuguese force was withdrawn, Sumbhajee attacked Colaba. Mannajee invoked the aid of the Peishwa, who compelled Sumbhajee to raise the siege, and received the Angrian forts of Koolta and Rajmachee in return, while Mannajee proclaimed his allegiance to the Peishwa, and henceforth was secure under his protection. The Portuguese, incensed against Mannajee, who had broken his promises to cede them certain districts in return for their assistance in capturing Colaba, joined hands with Sumbhajee Angria against him. This brought down upon them the hostility of the Mahratta court, who, after two years' severe fighting, expelled them from Salsette and all their possessions in the neighbourhood of Bombay, while the English looked on at the contest waged at their doors with indifference.

In order to strengthen themselves against the Dutch, the Portuguese had ceded Bombay to the English, and then, by their bad faith in retaining Salsette and Thana, they had opened a sore that never was healed. By espousing the quarrel of Mannajee they had earned the enmity of Sumbhajee; and by joining in Sumbhajee's quarrel against Mannajee they had brought down on themselves the formidable power of the Peishwa. Before long, Sumbhajee turned against them again, and they were left without a single ally to struggle as they could. Their intervention in Angrian quarrels was the final cause of the downfall of Portuguese power on the West coast.

The old political landmarks were fast disappearing. Everywhere the Mogul power was crumbling to pieces, and new principalities were being formed. The Peishwa had shaken off his allegiance to Satara, and his armies were making his authority felt all over Hindostan and the Deccan; while Mahratta rule was being established in Guzerat by the Gaicowar. The Dutch and French had ceased to make progress; the Portuguese power was on the wane; the *Seedee* was losing territory under the attacks of Mannajee and the Peishwa, while the Angrian power was divided. Meanwhile, the Company's position on the West coast was steadily improving. European pirates had ceased to haunt the Indian seas; Mannajee Angria found it necessary to maintain good relations with the English, though occasional acts of hostility showed that he was not to be trusted; while the Peishwa, whose aims were directed inland, had no quarrel with them, and concluded a treaty with Bombay.

Trade was flourishing, though the piracies of Sumbhajee Angria, in spite of his feud with Mannajee, caused losses from time to time. The English ships, better manned and better found, no longer contented themselves with repelling attacks, but boldly cruised in search of Sumbhajee's vessels, capturing them or driving them to seek refuge in their fortified harbours.

To relate in detail all the encounters that took place would be tedious; but some of them may be mentioned, in order to give an idea of the warfare that went on for thirty years after Boone's relinquishment of office.

In October, 1730, intelligence having been received of Angrian *gallivats* cruising north of Bombay, some Bombay *gallivats* were sent out, and after a smart action captured three of them, each carrying five guns. A month later, the *Bombay* and *Bengal* galleys were attacked off Colaba by four *grabs* and fifteen *gallivats*. There was a calm at the time: the hostile *grabs* were towed under the galleys' stern and opened a heavy fire. The galleys were only able to reply with small arm fire, and suffered severely. Several attempts to board were repelled, when an unlucky shot exploded two barrels of musket cartridges on board the *Bengal*. The quarter-deck was blown up, and, in the confusion, the enemy boarded and carried the ship. The first lieutenant, although wounded, jumped overboard and swam to the *Bombay*, which was also in evil plight. A similar explosion had occurred, killing the captain, the first lieutenant, and many of the crew. At this juncture came a welcome breeze, bringing up the *Victory grab*, which had witnessed the fight without being able to take part in it, and the Angrians drew off. No less than eighty Europeans were lost to the Company in this action.

In January, 1732, the *Ockham*, East Indiaman, coming up the coast with a light wind, was beset, off Dabul, by an Angrian squadron of five *grabs* and three *gallivats*. At sunset they came within shot, and a little harmless cannonading took place at long range, till dark. At one in the morning, the moon having risen, they bore down again and attacked the *Ockham* in their favourite manner, astern. For some time the East Indiaman was exposed to the fire of ten nine-pounders, to which it could only reply with two stern-chasers. Captain Jobson, finding his rigging much cut up, and seeing that the loss of a mast would probably entail the loss of his ship, determined to entice them to close quarters, in the good breeze that was springing up.

The plan was explained to the crew, who were in good heart, and encouraged by a promise of two months' pay. Every gun was manned, while the fire of the two stern-chasers was allowed to slacken, as if ammunition was running short. The bait took; the *grabs* drew up on the *Ockham's* quarter, with their crews cheering and sounding trumpets.

At a cable's distance the *Ockham* suddenly tacked; and as she gathered way on her new course, she was in the midst of the *grabs*, firing into them round shot and grape, together with volleys of small arms. This unexpected manoeuvre made the Angrians draw off, and the *Ockham* resumed her course. At daybreak, only four *grabs* were in chase, the fifth having evidently suffered severe injuries. A stiff breeze had sprung up, and the crew were eager for another bout, so the *Ockham* tacked again, and stood for the *grabs*. But they had had enough of it, and evaded coming to close quarters. Their best chances of successes lay in calms and light airs. With an antagonist like Jobson, in a good stiff wind, the odds were against them; they had lost many men; so after hovering round for some hours they made off to Severndroog.

In 1734, the *Coolee* rovers, who infested the coast of Guzerat, gave much trouble. Their stronghold was at Sultanpore, on the River Coorla, and they enjoyed the protection of several wealthy persons who shared in their plunder. A squadron under Captain Radford Nunn was sent against them, which captured five armed vessels and burnt fourteen more. To save others from capture they burnt about fifty more small sailing-boats themselves. Six months later, ten more of their boats were burnt and two captured. Under these blows they were quiet for a time.

In December, 1735, a valuable ship fell into Sumbhajee Angria's hands, owing to the bad behaviour of its captain. The *Derby*, East Indiaman, bringing a great cargo of naval stores from England, and the usual treasure for investment, was due to arrive in Bombay in November. The captain, Anselme, was a schemer, and wished to remain in India for a year, instead of returning to England at once, as had been arranged. Accordingly, he lingered a month in Johanna, and shaped his course northward along the African coast. Thence getting a fair wind which would have brought him directly to Bombay, without running the risk of working along the Malabar coast, he, instead, steered for the latitude of Goa, and thence crept northwards, making as much delay as possible, so as not to reach Bombay till January.

On the 26th December, an Angrian squadron of five *grabs* and four *gallivats* bore down on the *Derby*, off Severndroog, and engaged in their favourite way of attacking a big ship, astern. There was little wind, and the *Derby* would neither stay nor wear. Only two guns could be brought to bear at first; there were no guns mounted in the gun-room, and no encouragement was given to the crew. Two years before, the directors had authorized the captains of outward-bound ships, when exposed to a serious attack, to hoist two treasure chests on deck, for distribution, after the engagement, to the ship's company, in order to encourage them in making a good resistance. The captains of homeward-bound ships were empowered to promise £2000 to their crews in the same circumstances.

Nothing of the kind was done by Anselme. The crew, discontented, fought with little spirit; many of them refused to stand to their guns. The main and mizzen masts were shot away, seven men, including the first mate, were killed, five were dangerously, and a number more slightly, wounded. Still, many of the officers and men were willing to continue the fight, but were overruled by the captain, who insisted on surrender, and the *Derby* with 115 prisoners, of whom two were ladies, was carried into Severndroog.

No such loss had befallen the Company for many years. The much-needed naval stores went to equip Angria's fleet, and the money for the season's investment was lost. The whole Bombay trade was dislocated. Angria, desirous of peace, opened negotiations. The Council, wishing to redeem the prisoners, offered a six months' truce, and, after eleven months of captivity the prisoners were sent to Bombay, with the exception of three who took service with Angria.

In December, 1736, the *King George* and three other vessels captured a large *grab* belonging to Sumbhajee Angria, together with 120 prisoners. A Surat ship that had been taken was also recovered.

The year 1738 was an anxious one in Bombay. The Mahrattas were occupied with the siege of Bassein, which was defended with desperate valour by the Portuguese. Sumbhajee's vessels were active on the coast, and Mannajee was restless and untrustworthy. Commodore Bagwell, with four of the Company's best ships, the *Victory, King George, Princess Caroline*, and *Resolution*, was sent to cruise against Sumbhajee, while Captain Inchbird was deputed on a friendly mission to Mannajee. On the 22nd December, Bagwell sighted Sumbhajee's fleet of nine *grabs* and thirteen *gallivats* coming out of Gheriah. He gave chase, and forced them to take refuge in the mouth of the Rajapore River, where they anchored.

Bagwell, ignorant of the navigation, and with his crews badly afflicted with scurvy, boldly bore down on them; on which they cut their cables and ran into the river. Before they could get out of shot, he was able to pour in several broadsides at close range, killing Angria's chief admiral, and inflicting much damage. Fearing to lose some of his ships in the shoal water, he was obliged to draw off, having had one midshipman killed.

Mannajee at once took advantage of Sumbhajee's temporary discomfiture to attack and capture Caranjah from the Portuguese. Then, elated at his success, and in spite of his own professions of friendship, he seized three unarmed Bombay trading ships and two belonging to Surat. To punish him, Captain Inchbird was sent with a small squadron, and seized eight of his fighting *gallivats*, together with a number of fishing-boats. Negotiations were opened, broken off, and renewed, during which Mannajee insolently hoisted his flag on the island of Elephanta. With the Mahratta army close at hand in Salsette, the Bombay Council dared not push matters to extremity; so, invoking the help of Chimnajee Appa, the Peishwa's brother, they patched up a peace with Mannajee. At the same time, Bombay succeeded in making a treaty of friendship with the Peishwa, which secured, to the English, trading facilities in his dominions.

While this was going on, a Dutch squadron of seven ships of war and seven sloops attacked Gheriah, and were beaten off. A little later, Sumbhajee took the *Jupiter*, a French ship of forty guns, with four hundred slaves on board. To English, Dutch, French, and Portuguese alike, his fortresses were impregnable.

In January, 1740, a gallant action was fought by the *Harrington*, Captain Jenkins. The *Harrington* was returning from a voyage to China, and, in coming up the coast, had joined company with the *Pulteney*, *Ceres*, and *Halifax*. Between Tellicherry and Bombay they were attacked by fifteen sail of Angria's fleet. Four *grabs* ran alongside the *Harrington*, but were received with such a well-directed fire that they dropped astern. The four Company's ships then formed line abreast, and were attacked from astern by Angria's ships. The brunt of the fight fell on the *Harrington*. Jenkins had trained his crew, and was prepared for this method of attack. After five hours of heavy firing the Angrian ships drew off, showing confusion and loss.

At daylight the next morning they attacked again. The *Ceres* had fallen to leeward, and three *grabs* attacked her, while three more bore down on the *Harrington* to windward. Disregarding his own attackers, Jenkins bore down on the assailants of the *Ceres*, and drove them off; then, hauling his wind, he awaited the attack of the others. The three leeward *grabs* were towed up within range, and for the next two or three hours the *Harrington* engaged all six, almost single-handed. The wind had fallen; the *Ceres* and *Halifax* were out of gunshot; the *Pulteney* alone was able to give assistance at long range. So well served were the *Harrington's* guns that she inflicted more damage than she received, and, by ten o'clock, four of the *grabs* gave up the contest and were towed away to windward.

The other two *grabs* continued the action for some time, till they also were towed out of action. The two squadrons, just out of gunshot of each other, consulted among themselves. Jenkins found he had only seven rounds left for his big guns, and his consorts, which were more lightly armed, were in little better plight to renew the combat. Still, he put a good face on it, showing no unwillingness to continue the fight; and, on a breeze springing up, the Angrians drew off, leaving the East Indiamen to pursue their voyage. Only one man on board the *Harrington* was wounded, though the ship was much knocked about. Jenkins was much commended for his skill and courage, and two years later we find him acting as Commodore of the Company's fleet at Bombay.

Three weeks later, Sumbhajee's fleet of five *grabs* and some *gallivats* appeared off Bombay, and cruised off the mouth of the harbour, as if inviting attack. Commodore Langworth, with the *Pulteney, Trial, Neptune's Prize*, a bomb-*ketch*, and five of the largest *gallivats*, was sent out. The Angrian fleet stood away to the southward, followed by Langworth. The demonstration was a trick to draw off the Bombay fighting ships. When they were well out of the way, Sumbhajee made a sudden attack on Mannajee's territories with two thousand men and forty or fifty *gallivats*. Sumbhajee had gained over a number of Mannajee's officers, and Alibagh, Thull, and Sagurgurh fell into his hands at once. He attacked Chaul, but was beaten off by the Portuguese, and then laid siege to Colaba.

Mannajee was at once reduced to great straits. Half his garrison were untrustworthy, and his water supply was cut off. In his distress he appealed to Bombay for assistance. Though the council bore him little good will, they recognized that it was better to maintain him in Colaba than to allow Sumbhajee to establish himself there; so, in great haste, the *Halifax*, a small country ship, the *Futteh Dowlet grab*, the *Triumph, Prahm*, and the *Robert* galley were equipped and sent down, under Captain Inchbird, arriving just in time to save the place. Water was supplied to the garrison, and Bombardier Smith, together with gunner's mate Watson, a mortar and plenty of ammunition were put into the fort. Sumbhajee's batteries were much damaged by the shells from the mortar, his camp was bombarded by Inchbird, and his *gallivats* forced to run for Severndroog.

This prompt action of the Bombay Council upset Sumbhajee's plans. He addressed remonstrances to the council, offering to restore the *Anne*, which he had taken some months before. A week later, a Mahratta force, from Salsette, under the Peishwa's son, Ballajee Bajee Rao, appeared on the scene, attacked Sumbhajee's camp, destroyed some of his batteries, killing a number of his men, and taking prisoner his half-brother, Toolajee.

In his distress, Sumbhajee tried to come to terms with Mannajee. Each distrusted the other, and both were afraid of the Peishwa. At this juncture the death of the Peishwa was announced. Ballajee Bajee Rao was obliged to return to Satara, and Sumbhajee was allowed to retreat, after making peace with the Mahrattas. The promptitude and energy with which the English had come to the assistance of Mannajee raised them greatly in the esteem of the new Peishwa, and strengthened the bonds of the alliance.

Mannajee now found it expedient to make a solid peace with the English. The new Peishwa had his hands full at Satara. The only power able to afford him ready protection against Sumbhajee was the English, the value of whose friendship he had lately experienced. So he sent agents to Bombay, offering to pay a sum of *Rs.*7500, on restitution of the *gallivats* taken from him by Inchbird the year before. On this basis a peace was made.

At the same time, the Portuguese, whose power and resources were fast diminishing, recognized the difficulty of retaining the isolated fortress of Chaul. They offered it first to the Dutch and then to the English, but the dangerous gift was refused by both. Finally they made it over to the Peishwa by agreement.[1]

While these things were going on, the *Antelope, gallivat*, fell a prey to the *Coolee* rovers of Sultanpore. Through the treachery of the pilot it was run ashore. The crew defended themselves gallantly, but in the course of the action the ship blew up, and ten Europeans, two *sepoys*, and two lascars were killed.

In view of the losses he had sustained, Sumbhajee Angria now tried to patch up a peace with Bombay. In order to test his sincerity, he was required, as a preliminary step, to restore the English prisoners he held. Just then he scored a success against the Portuguese, from whom he captured two fine *grabs* and a convoy; so the negotiation came to a standstill. But his fortunes were declining, his people were leaving his service, while Mannajee, protected by the Peishwa and the English,

---
1. September, 1740.

was increasing in power; so he again addressed the Bombay governor, in a letter beginning 'For thirty years we have been at war.' But it was soon discovered that his object was to have his hands free to attack Mannajee, and his overtures came to nothing.

In May, 1743, he captured the Bombay ketch *Salamander*, off Colaba, but before it could be carried off it was rescued by some of Mannajee's ships from Chaul, and restored to Bombay. Very shortly afterwards, Sumbhajee died, and was succeeded by his half-brother, Toolajee. The reputation of the English in Bombay was now so good, that a quarrel between Mannajee and the Peishwa was referred to them for arbitration.

The predatory policy of the Angrian family did not suffer in the hands of Toolajee. Within a few weeks of Sumbhajee's death, his squadron fought a prolonged action with the *Warwick* and *Montagu*, East Indiamen, and carried off five small vessels sailing under their convoy. Commodore Hough in the *Restoration*, together with the *Bombay grab*, was at once sent down the coast, and found seven Angrian *grabs* with a number of *gallivats*, which he forced to take shelter under the guns of Severndroog. A year later, the *Princess Augusta* from Bencoolen was captured by Toolajee, and taken into Gheriah. After plundering it, Toolajee found it was too poor a sailer to be of use to him, so he allowed the Bombay Council to redeem it for *Rs.*8000.

Meanwhile, war with France had broken out, and the capture of Madras by La Bourdonnais dealt a severe blow to English prestige. The restless Mannajee began stopping and plundering small native craft belonging to Bombay, with the intention, no doubt, of flying at higher game in time. Reprisals were at once ordered, and a vessel of Mannajee's was captured. This brought him to reason, and the vessel was released on his signing a bond to make good the losses he had caused. The loss of Madras was telling against the English, everywhere. In Bengal the Mahrattas seized the Cossimbazaar flotilla bound for Calcutta, valued at four *lakhs* of *rupees*. Mannajee still continued to be troublesome, till the *Seedee*, taking advantage of the situation, attacked and captured Thull, which kept him quiet for a time.

Considerable anxiety was caused in Bombay, at this time, by the appearance of three French men-of-war cruising on the coast, with the evident intention of waylaying the Company's ships from Europe. One of them was a fifty-gun ship, and there was nothing in Bombay harbour to cope with her. To meet the difficulty, a large number of fishing-boats were sent out, each with an English sailor on board, to creep along the coast and warn all incoming ships. In spite of these precautions, the *Anson* missed the boats sent to warn her, and was attacked by the French *Apollo* and *Anglesea* within sight of the harbour. Captain Foulis defended himself long enough to enable him to send off the dispatches and treasure he carried, in his boats, before he was forced to surrender.[2] The directors bestowed on him a gratuity of £400 for his able conduct.

Fortunately for Bombay, Toolajee Angria's energies were at this time directed against Canara, where in two successive expeditions he sacked Mangalore and Honore, carrying off a large booty.

In October, 1749, Toolajee, who for some time had been giving little trouble, inflicted a severe loss on the Bombay marine. The *Restoration* was the most efficient ship at the council's disposal. It had been commanded by Captain Hough, a bold and resolute man, who had done good service in her, attacking Angria's ships and chasing them into their fortified harbours. She carried seventy-five European seamen, sixteen lascars, and thirty soldiers—unruly fellows who wanted a firm hand over them. Hough had fallen ill, and the command was given to Captain Thomas Leake, an irresolute man, not fitted to command such, a crew. They very soon fell into disorder. While coming up the coast from Goa they were attacked by Toolajee's fleet of five *grabs*, accompanied by a swarm of *gallivats*.

From noon till dark the *Restoration* was surrounded and cannonaded. Her guns were so badly served that they inflicted little or no damage, while her own sails and rigging were badly cut about. During the night, the action was fitfully continued, her ammunition being lavishly and uselessly expended. Toolajee himself was present, and had a number of European gunners with him. At noon the next day his *grabs* edged down again, fell aboard the *Restoration*, and boarded. On this, the colours were struck, Leake ran below, an example that was followed by his crew, and the ship was taken. When they were released, some months afterwards, the council, after due inquiry, decided that Leake and his officers should not serve the Company again till the Directors' pleasure was known.

Meanwhile, the *Coolees* of Guzerat had become very troublesome. In 1749, they captured a Bengal ship with *Rs.*60,000 in hard cash on board, and a cargo of nearly equal value. Their depredations continuing, the Dutch proposed joint action against them; so, in December, 1750, a joint Dutch and English squadron forced the defences of the

---
2. 2nd September, 1747.

Coorla River, burnt and captured twenty-three of their vessels, and reduced them to quietness for a time.

Toolajee had now become very powerful. From Cutch to Cochin his vessels swept the coast in greater numbers than Conajee had ever shown, and cruised defiantly off Bombay harbour. But for the presence of four King's ships on the coast, Bombay trade would have suffered severely. When Boscawen left Indian waters,[3] after receiving over Madras from the French, he detached four ships, the *Vigilant*, *Tartar*, *Ruby*, and *Syren*, to cruise on the West coast, under Commodore Lisle. For two years, the protection afforded by Lisle's squadron gave some security to the Bombay coast trade. As the small sailing boats, in which the coast trade was carried on, made their way under convoy of the King's ships, Angria's squadrons hovered round to pick up stragglers, and several slight encounters took place. The superior sailing powers of the Mahratta vessels enabled them to keep out of range of the big guns, while they snatched prizes within sight of the men-of-war.

Thus, in February, 1750, three small traders were snapped up, while under convoy of the *Ruby*, by an Angrian squadron that hung on their tracks for four days, between Bombay and Vingorla. In October, the *Tartar*, with twenty-six sail under convoy, was followed for three days, between Bombay and Surat, by eleven Angrian *gallivats*, and lost one of the number. Three weeks later, the *Syren's* convoy was attacked in the same waters by thirteen Angrian vessels, which were beaten off without loss.

In March, 1751, thirty-six trading vessels, under convoy of the *Vigilant* and *Ruby*, were attacked by six Angrian vessels, which behaved with great boldness. Instead of devoting themselves to the traders, they bore down on the *Ruby*, and opened fire at close range, with great guns and small arms. Before long an Angrian *grab* was seen to be on fire, and in a short time the after part blew up. Several pieces of mast were blown on board the *Ruby*, tearing her sails and wounding two men. The *grab* sunk, and her consorts made off. Hardly had Lisle's squadron sailed for England[4] when the council sustained a loss in the *Swallow* sloop, which was taken by Toolajee, together with a convoy of rice-boats.

The great benefit conferred on the coast trade by Lisle's squadron taught the directors the necessity of a change of policy. Hitherto their fighting ships had been utilized to carry cargoes along the coast, a

---

3. November, 1749.
4. November, 1751.

practice that greatly hampered their action. They now determined on keeping ships for fighting only; so they ordered the building of the *Protector*, a forty-gun ship, and the *Guardian*, a sloop. The two new ships left Sheerness in the winter of 1751, commanded by Captains Cheyne and James, and the most stringent orders were sent with them that they were to carry no cargoes, and were to be kept on the Malabar coast as long as Angria should keep the sea. During the next three years, the *Protector* and *Guardian* did much useful work, convoying the coasting trade, and offering battle to Angria's ships whenever they met them.

CHAPTER 11

The Downfall of Angria

In the beginning of 1754, the Dutch suffered a severe loss at Toolajee's hands. A vessel loaded with ammunition was taken, and two large ships were blown up after a stiff fight, in which Toolajee had two three-masted *grabs* sunk and a great number of men killed. Six months later, Toolajee sent an agent to Bombay to propose terms of accommodation. They were terms to which a conciliatory answer, at least, would have been returned in Conajee Angria's time. The council's reply betrays a consciousness of increased strength. "Can you imagine that the English will ever submit to take passes of any Indian nation? This they cannot do. We grant passes, but would take none from anybody." Toolajee was told that if he was in earnest in desiring peace, he should return the vessels he had taken, and send men of figure and consequence to treat, instead of the obscure individual through whom his overtures had come.

In spite of this peremptory reply, Toolajee continued to make half-hearted proposals for peace. The fact was that he was now at open war with the Peishwa, who had made himself master of the Concan, with the exception of the coastline. According to Orme, Toolajee had cut off the noses of the agents sent by the Peishwa to demand the tribute formerly paid to Satara. The Poonah *Durbar* were so incensed against him that they were determined on his destruction, though without the assistance of the English they had little expectation of success against his coast fortresses. The Bombay Council was ready enough to join in the undertaking, but was unwilling to take immediate action. This unwillingness was apparently due to their desire to see order first restored in Surat, where affairs had fallen into great disorder in the general break-up of Mogul rule.

The Mahratta Court at Poona had been close observers of the long war waged in the Carnatic between the English and French. They had seen Madras taken, only to be regained by diplomacy, and after the English had been foiled at Pondicherry. They had witnessed the rise of French power under Dupleix; rulers deposed and others set up, in the Deccan and the Carnatic, by French arms; and then, when Mahomed Ali, the rightful ruler of the Carnatic, was at his last gasp, they had seen his cause espoused by the English, and one humiliation after another inflicted on French armies, till at last the French were forced to recognize Mahomed Ali's title, while a powerful English squadron and a King's regiment had been sent out to make good the claim. The good relations established between the Peishwa's government and Bombay by the treaty of 1739, had been strengthened since the arrival of Mr. Richard Bourchier, as governor, in 1750; the fighting in the Carnatic had raised the military reputation of the English, while their support of Mahomed Ali, whom the Mahrattas styled 'their master,' had greatly increased the esteem in which they were held.

When it was definitely known that hostilities between the English and French were at an end, Ramajee Punt, the *Sirsoobah* of the Concan, was dispatched to Bombay to concert measures against Toolajee. Mr. Bourchier was urged to summon the King's ships from Madras to co-operate with the Peishwa's forces.

To await the arrival of Watson's squadron from Madras would have lost the favourable season before the monsoon, so it was determined to fit out at once what ships were in the harbour, and send them under Commodore William James. Articles of agreement were drawn up, by which it was settled that Severndroog, Anjanvel, and Jyeghur should be attacked by the Mahrattas, while the English engaged to keep the sea, and prevent Toolajee's fleet from throwing succours into the places attacked. A division of the spoils between the victors was agreed on, by which the English were to receive Bankote and Himmutghur, with five villages, in perpetual sovereignty. The Peishwa's fleet was to be under James's orders, and he was instructed to give all the assistance in his power, but not to lend any of his people, except a few to point the guns.

Very little is accurately known of James's career before his entry into the East India Company's service. He was born in Pembrokeshire in humble circumstances, and went to sea at an early age. According to one account, he served in Hawke's ship, but, wherever his training was received, it had made him a first-rate seaman. In 1747, he entered the Company's marine service, being then about twenty-six years of age.

In 1751, he sailed from England in command of the *Guardian* sloop, one of the two men-of-war built by the directors for the protection of Bombay trade. His services against the coast pirates, during the next two years, procured his advancement to the post of commodore at Bombay, and it was soon remarked that the sailing of the *Protector*, on which his flag was now hoisted, had greatly improved by the changes he had made. By his capture of Severndroog, now to be related, he became famous. He played his part at the capture of Gheriah, and, in the following year, when the news of the disaster at Calcutta became known in Bombay, he was sent down in the *Revenge*, with four hundred men, to join the force sent up from Madras under Watson and Clive. Off Calicut he encountered the French ship *Indien*, carrying twenty-four guns and over two hundred men, and captured her. He afterwards joined the board of directors, was created a baronet, had a seat in Parliament, and, in time, became chairman of the Company. Sterne, in the last year of his life, formed a close friendship with Mr. and Mrs. James, and, a few days before he died, recommended his daughter Lydia to their care.

On the 22nd March, 1755, James sailed from Bombay in the *Protector*, forty guns, having with him the *Swallow*, sixteen guns, the *Viper*-bombketch, and the *Triumph prahm*. The following day, he sighted an Angrian squadron of seven *grabs* and eleven *gallivats*, which he chased for a couple of hours without success. Two days later, he was joined off Chaul by the Peishwa's fleet, consisting of seven *grabs*, two *batellas*, and about forty *gallivats*. To James's annoyance, he found his allies in no hurry to get on. Twice they insisted on landing, lingering for over three days in one place.

On the 29th, Severndroog was sighted, and Angria's fleet of seven *grabs* and ten *gallivats* was observed coming out. The signal to chase was made, but obeyed with little alacrity by the Peishwa's people, though experience had shown that they could outsail the Bombay ships. James gave chase with his little squadron, his Mahratta allies being left, by evening, hull down, astern. The Angrians made prodigious exertions to escape, hanging out turbans and clothing to catch every breath of air. All the following day the ineffectual chase continued, the *Protector* outsailing its own consorts, and losing sight altogether of its Mahratta allies. Finding it useless to persevere, James hauled his wind, and stood to the northward for Severndroog, which he had left far behind in the chase. Here he found Ramajee Punt, who had landed a few men, and entrenched himself at about two miles from the nearest fort, with a single four-pounder gun.

The harbour of Severndroog[1] is formed by a slight indentation in the coast and a small rocky islet about a quarter of a mile from the mainland, on which was the Severndroog fort, with walls fifty feet high, and, in many places, parapets cut out of the solid rock; the whole armed with about fifty guns. On the mainland, opposite to Severndroog, was another fort. Fort Gova, armed with, about forty-four guns, while southwards of Gova were two smaller forts on a small promontory, Futteh Droog and Kanak Droog, armed with twenty guns each.

James at once saw that the reduction of the different forts by the Peishwa's troops would be a matter of months, even if he was able to keep out succours from the sea, which the monsoon would render impossible; so, in spite of the council's orders, he resolved on taking matters into his own hands. He had been brought up in a good school, and knew that, to match a ship against a fort with success, it was necessary to get as close as possible, and overpower it with weight of metal. After taking the necessary soundings, on the 2nd April he stood in to four-fathom water, taking with him the *Viper* and *Triumph*, and bombarded Severndroog Fort. The Mahratta fleet gave no assistance, so the *Swallow* was detached to guard the southern entrance.

All day long the cannonade continued, till a heavy swell setting into the harbour, in the evening, obliged a cessation of fire. The fort fired briskly in return, but did little damage; while the Mahratta fleet lay off out of range, idle spectators of the conflict. At night came Ramajee Punt on board the *Protector*, bringing with him a deserter from the fort, who reported that the governor had been killed and a good deal of damage done. He told them that it was impossible to breach the side on which the *Protector's* fire was directed, as it was all solid rock.

In the morning, the *Protector* weighed and ran in again, James placing his ships between Severndroog and Gova. The flagship engaged Severndroog so closely that, by the small arm fire of men in the tops, and by firing two or three upper-deck guns at a time instead of in broadsides, the Severndroog gunners were hardly able to return a shot. With her lower-deck guns on the other side the *Protector* cannonaded the mainland forts, which also received the attention of the *Viper* and *Triumph*. It would be difficult to find a parallel to this instance of a single ship and two bomb-*ketches* successfully engaging four forts at once, that far outnumbered them in guns; but so good were James's

1. Properly Suvarna Droog, 'the Golden Fortress.'

arrangements that neither his ships nor his men suffered harm.

Soon after midday a magazine exploded in Severndroog; the conflagration spread, and, before long, men, women, and children were seen taking to their boats, and escaping to the mainland. Numbers of them were intercepted and taken by the *Swallow* and the Mahratta *gallivats*. The bombardment of the mainland forts was continued till night, and resumed the following morning, till about ten o'clock, when all three hauled down their colours. Thus, in forty-eight hours, did James by his vigorous action reduce this Angrian stronghold that was second only to Gheriah in strength. The Mahrattas were never slow at seizing any advantage that had been won by others, as was shown a few months later at Gheriah; but on this occasion they were so struck by James's intrepidity that they refused to enter Gova without him.

The English flag was hoisted in all three forts, amid the cheers of the English sailors. It was then found that, by mismanagement, the governor of Gova had been allowed to escape over to Severndroog, and gallantly reoccupied it, with a small body of *sepoys*, hoping to hold out till assistance could reach him from Dabul. So the *Protector's* guns were set to work again, and, under cover of their fire, a party of seamen was landed, who hewed open the sally port with their axes and made themselves masters of the fort. Thus, in a few hours, and without losing a single man, had "the spirited resolution of Commodore James destroyed the timorous prejudices which had for twenty years been entertained of the impracticability of reducing any of Angria's fortified harbours."

The whole success of the expedition had been due to James, and the Peishwa's officers ungrudgingly acknowledged the fact, as well as the bad behaviour of their own people. "I have learnt with particular satisfaction that the fleet your Honor sent to the assistance of Ramajee Punt have by their courage and conduct reduced Severndroog, the suddenness of which transcends my expectations; and I allow myself incapable of sufficiently commending their merit," wrote the Peishwa's commander-in-chief to Bourchier. Ramajee Punt wrote in similar terms, and sent a dress of honour to James. In their elation, the Peishwa's officers wished to complete the destruction of Angria without delay. Bankote was surrendered to them without firing a shot, and a demonstration was made against Rutnaghiri.

But the council was cautious, and forbade James to risk his ships. The Mahrattas offered him two *lakhs* of *rupees* if he would support them in attacking Dabul, but he dared not exceed his orders again, and returned to Bombay. The success of a second *coup-de-main* could not be relied on, and a repulse would have restored Toolajee's drooping spirits, and made future success more difficult. The soldiers Bombay had lent to Madras were no longer required, so James was sent there in the *Protector*, to bring them back after the monsoon.

In the end of October, an unexpected accession of force, from England, reached Bombay. In the suspension of arms that had been concluded at Madras between the English and French, Carnatic affairs alone were made the subject of agreement. Bussy, with a French force, remained in the Deccan, engaged in extending the Nizam's influence, a proceeding that was viewed with alarm by the Peishwa. With the object of expelling the French from the Deccan, the English Government sent out to Bombay a force of seven hundred men, to act against Bussy, in concert with the Mahratta government. The command was to be taken by Lieutenant-Colonel Scott, the Company's engineer-general at Madras.

The directors had also sent Clive to Bombay to act as second in command to Scott. But Scott had died, in the meantime, and the *Doddington*, East Indiaman, bringing the directors' instructions to the Bombay Council, had been wrecked near the Cape. Before the middle of November, Watson's squadron arrived, in furtherance of the Deccan project, together with James, in the *Protector*, bringing two hundred and fifty-five Bombay soldiers from Madras. Clive, alone, knew of the directors' plan for the Deccan, and urged it on the council. Ramajee Punt was in Bombay urging them to complete the destruction of Angria, and inviting them to take possession of Bankote;[2] so they decided to devote themselves to Gheriah, on the grounds that the Deccan expedition would be an infringement of the late agreement with the French.

Seeing that nothing was to be done in the Deccan, Watson tendered the services of his squadron to assist in the reduction of Gheriah, and Clive offered to command the land forces. James was sent down in the *Protector*, with the *Revenge* and *Guardian*, with Sir William Hewitt, Watson's flag lieutenant, to reconnoitre and take soundings. Nothing was known of Gheriah. It was supposed to be as high, and as strong as Gibraltar. Like that celebrated fortress, it stood on rocky ground at the end of a promontory, connected with the mainland by a narrow neck of ground, at the month of a small estuary. James found

---

2. Bankote was made over on the 6th December, and the British flag hoisted there on the 10th January, 1756.

that it was less formidable than it had been represented, and that large ships could go close in. To prevent Toolajee's ships from escaping, the *Bridgewater, Kingsfisher,* and *Revenge* were sent to blockade the place till the expedition was ready to start.

On the 11th February, the whole force was assembled off Gheriah, a greater armament than had yet ever left Bombay harbour. In addition to Watson's squadron of six vessels, four of them line-of-battle ships, and displaying the flags of two admirals, the Company's marine made a brave show of eighteen ships, large and small, carrying two hundred and fourteen guns, besides twenty fishing-boats to land troops with, each carrying a swivel-gun in the bows. Between them they carried eight hundred European and six hundred native troops. With Watson also went Captain Hough, superintendent of the Company's marine, as representative of the council.

Part of the instructions given to Clive and Hough by the council will bear repeating.

> It is probable that Toolajee Angria may offer to capitulate, and possibly offer a sum of money; but you are to consider that this fellow is not on a footing with any prince in the known world, he being a pirate in whom no confidence can be put, not only taking, burning, and destroying ships of all nations, but even the vessels belonging to the natives, which have his own passes, and for which he has annually collected large sums of money. Should he offer any sum of money it must be a very great one that will pay us for the many rich ships he has taken (which we can't enumerate), besides the innumerable other smaller vessels; but we well remember the *Charlotte* bound from hence to China, belonging to Madras; the *William* belonging to Bombay, from Bengal; the *Severn*, a Bengal freight ship for Bussorah, value nine or ten *lakhs* of *rupees*; the *Derby* belonging to the Honourable Company, with the *grab Restoration*, value *Rs.*5,22,743-4-6; the sloop *Pilot* and the *Augusta*; also the *Dadaboy* from Surat, *Rose* from Mangalore, *grab Anne* from Gombroon, *Benjimolly* from the Malabar coast, and *Futte Dowlat* from Muscat.

The council were desirous of getting Toolajee into their own custody, fearful that, if left in Mahratta hands, he would be set free before long, and the work would have to be done over again.

Before the expedition left Bombay, a council of war was held, to decide on the division of spoils, between the sea and land forces. Such agreements were common enough, on such occasions, in order to prevent subsequent disputes and individual plundering. In settling the shares of the officers, the council decided that Clive and Chalmers, who was next to Clive in command of the troops, should have shares equal to that of two captains of King's ships. To this Clive objected that, though as lieutenant-colonel, his share would, according to custom, be equal to that of a naval captain, on this occasion, as commander-in-chief of the troops, it should be greater, and ought not to be less than that of Rear-Admiral Pocock. The council of war refused to agree to this, as the naval officers, who formed the majority, could not be brought to consent. Like Drake, who would rather diminish his own portion than leave any of his people unsatisfied, Watson undertook to 'give the colonel such a part of his share as will make it equal to Rear-Admiral Pocock's;' and this was duly entered in the proceedings.

In the division of spoils, no mention is made of their Mahratta allies. They were left out of account altogether, and the reason is not far to seek. Experience had shown that, in the coming military operations, the Mahrattas would count for nothing. All the hard knocks would fall on the English, and it was but fair that they should have the prize-money; the Mahrattas would gain a substantial benefit in the possession of Gheriah, which was to be made over to them after capture.

The arrangements for the command of the troops showed that the lessons of the last ten years of warfare against the French had borne fruit. The command was left to those who made it their profession. Henceforth we hear no more of factors and writers strutting about in uniform, calling themselves colonels and captains for a few weeks, and then returning to their ledgers. We have done with the Midfords and the Browns. Out of the thirteen years he had served the Company, Clive had been a soldier for eleven. He had definitely abandoned his civil position, and had embraced a military career, and his merits had been recognized by the grant of a lieutenant-colonel's commission from the king. The subordinate military officers also had improved. The worst of them had been weeded out, and many of them had learned their business under Lawrence in the Carnatic. Though much unnecessary interference still went on in quarters, they were left unfettered in the command of their men in the field.

A few hours after leaving Bombay, the expedition was overtaken by despatches from Bourchier, with intelligence that the Mahrattas were treating with Toolajee. On reaching Gheriah, they found the

Mahratta army encamped against it, and Ramajee Punt himself came off to tell the commanders that, with a little patience, the fort would surrender without firing a shot, as Toolajee was already in their hands and ready to treat. Alarmed at the great armament coming against him, and cowed by recent reverses, Toolajee had come as a suppliant into the Mahratta camp to try if, by finesse and chicanery, he might escape utter destruction, while, in Gheriah, he had left his brother-in-law with orders to defend it to the last. The Peishwa's officers, on their side, were anxious to get the place into their hands without admitting the English to any share of the booty; a design that was at once seen through by Hough and Watson.

Ramajee promised to bring Toolajee with him the following day, to show that he was not treating separately. Instead of doing so, he sent some subordinate officers, together with some of Toolajee's relations, with excuses, to keep Watson in play, while a large bribe was offered to Hough to induce him to persuade the admiral to suspend operations. Watson, who had already summoned the fort to surrender, let them know that he would not wait very long. They were taken to view the ship with its tiers of heavy guns, and, as a grim hint of what might be expected, he presented Toolajee's friends with a thirty-two pound shot as they left the ship.

At half-past one in the afternoon, the flag of truce having returned with the governor's refusal to surrender, signal was made to weigh, and the whole fleet stood into the harbour in three divisions, led by the *Kingsfisher*, sloop, and the *Bridgewater*. The inner line, nearest to the fort was formed by the line-of-battle ships and the *Protector*: the Company's *grabs* and bomb-*ketches*, with the *Guardian*, formed the second line, while the *gallivats* and small vessels formed a third, outer line. As the *Kingsfisher* came opposite the fort, a shot was fired at her. The signal was made to engage, and as each ship reached its station it came to an anchor, the inner line being within musket-shot of the fort. Across the mouth of the river, Toolajee's *grabs* were drawn up, among them being the *Restoration*, the capture of which, six years before, had caused so much heart-burning in Bombay.

As the heavy shot and shell came pouring in from over one hundred and fifty guns at close range, the Gheriah defenders manfully strove to repay the same with interest. But so terrific was the fire brought to bear on them, that it was impossible for them to lay their guns properly. In that February afternoon many a cruel outrage was expiated under that hail of iron. After two hours' firing, a shell set the *Restoration* on fire; it spread to the grabs, and before long the Angrian fleet,[3] that had been the terror of the coast for half a century, was in a blaze. The boats were ordered out, and, as evening came on, Clive was put on shore with the troops, and took up a position a mile and a half from the fort.

The Mahrattas joined him, and Toolajee, from whom the Peishwa's people had extorted a promise to surrender the fort, found means to send a letter into the place, warning his brother-in-law against surrender to the English. In the fort all was terror and dismay, though the governor manfully did his duty. From the burning shipping the flames spread to the *bazaars* and warehouses. All night the bomb-*ketches* threw in shells, while the conflagration continued. One square tower in the fort burned with such violence as to resemble a fabric of red-hot iron in a smithy.

Early next morning, Watson sent in a flag of truce again, but surrender was still refused, so the line-of-battle ships were warped in and recommenced firing; while Clive, who had approached the fort, battered it from the land side. At four in the afternoon a magazine in the fort blew up, and a white flag was hoisted. An officer was sent on shore, but the governor still attempted to evade surrender. He consented to admit five or six men into the fort to hoist English colours, but would not definitely surrender possession till next day. So fire was reopened, and in twenty minutes more the Angrian flag was hauled down for the last time, and the last shred of Angrian independence had ceased to exist.

Sixty men, under Captains Forbes and Buchanan, were marched up to hold the gate for the night. A body of the Peishwa's troops tried to gain admission, and offered the officers a bill on Bombay for a *lakh* of *rupees* to allow them to pass in. The offer was rejected, but the Peishwa's officer still continued to press in, till Forbes faced his men about, and, drawing his sword, swore he would cut him down if he persisted.

The following morning, the fort was taken possession of by Clive. The success had been gained at the cost of about twenty men killed and wounded.

Ramajee Punt at once made a formal demand for the fort to be given up to him. Watson, in return, demanded that Toolajee should be

---

3. Three three-masted ships carrying twenty guns each; nine two-masted, carrying from twelve to sixteen guns; thirteen *gallivats*, carrying from six to ten guns; thirty others unclassed; two on the stocks, one of them pierced for forty guns.

made over into English custody. Meanwhile, a hunt for the treasure secreted in different places went on. "Every day hitherto has been productive of some new discoveries of treasure, plate, and jewels, etc.," wrote Hough three days later. Altogether about one hundred and thirty thousand pounds' worth of gold, silver, and jewels were secured, and divided between the land and sea forces.

True to his promise, Watson sent Clive a thousand pounds to make his share equal to Pocock's. Clive sent it back again. He was satisfied with the acknowledgment of his claim, but would not take what came out of Watson's private purse. "Thus did these two gallant officers endeavour to outvie each other in mutual proofs of disinterestedness and generosity," wrote Ives in his narrative. A thousand pounds was a larger sum then than it would be now, and Clive was a poor man at the time, but he was never greedy of money. The incident justifies his boast, long afterwards, of his moderation when the treasures of Bengal were at his mercy. It is allowable to suppose that it strengthened the mutual respect of both, and facilitated their co-operation in Bengal, a year later. It was a fortunate thing for England that Watson was not a man of Matthews' stamp.

The Europeans in Toolajee's service appear to have left him before the attack began, as no mention is made of them; but ten Englishmen and three Dutchmen were found in the place, in a state of slavery, and released.

In delivering over Bankote, the Mahrattas had failed to give, with the fort, the five villages according to agreement. The council were desirous of having Toolajee in their own keeping, so they refused to give over Gheriah, and for some months a wrangle went on concerning the points in dispute. The council proposed that they should retain Gheriah and give up Bankote. The Peishwa taunted the council with breach of faith, and refused to give up Toolajee. The squabble was at last settled by the Mahrattas engaging to give ten villages near Bankote, and that Toolajee should not receive any territory within forty miles of the sea. On these conditions Gheriah was delivered over. Toolajee, instead of being given any territory, was kept a prisoner for the rest of his life. Some years afterwards, his sons made their escape, and sought refuge in Bombay.

With the fall of Gheriah, the heavy cloud that had so long hung over Bombay trade was dispelled. Thenceforward none but the smallest vessels had anything to fear on the coast south of Bombay, though another half-century elapsed before the Malwans were compelled to give up piracy. The Sanganians continued to be troublesome, at times, till they too were finally reduced to order in 1816, after more than one expedition had been sent against them. Persian Gulf piracy continued to flourish till 1835, when it was brought to an end by a happy combination of arms and diplomacy.

On Shooter's Hill, adjoining Woolwich Common, the tower of Severndroog, erected by James's widow to commemorate his great achievement, forms a conspicuous landmark in the surrounding country. Here, in sight of the spot where the bones of Kidd and his associates long hung in chains as a terror to evil-doers, there still lingers a breath of that long struggle against the Angrian pirates, and of its triumphant conclusion.

This far-seen monumental tow'r
Records the achievements of the brave,
And Angria's subjugated pow'r,
Who plundered on the Eastern wave.
    —*Walks through London,* David Hughson.

An Englishwoman in India Two Hundred Years Ago

On the 9th March, 1709, the *Loyall Bliss*, East Indiaman, Captain Hudson, left her anchorage in the Downs and sailed for Bengal. As passengers, she carried Captain Gerrard Cooke, his wife, a son and two daughters, together with a few soldiers. For many years Cooke had served the Company at Fort William, as gunner, an office that included the discharge of many incongruous duties. After a stay in England, he was now returning to Bengal, as engineer, with the rank of captain. The *Loyall Bliss* was a clumsy sailer, and made slow progress; so that August had come before she left the Cape behind her. Contrary winds and bad weather still detained her, and kept her westward of her course. By the middle of September, the south-west monsoon, on which they depended to carry them up the bay, had ceased to blow, so—"our people being a great many downe with the scurvy and our water being short, wee called a consultation of officers it being too late to pretend to get Bengali the season being come that the N.E. Trade wind being sett in and our people almost every man tainted with distemper," it was determined to make for Carwar and "endever to gett refresments there."

On the 7th October, they came to anchor in the little bay formed by the Carwar River. The next day, hearing of a French man-of-war being on the coast, they procured a pilot and anchored again under the guns of the Portuguese fort on the island of Angediva, where lay the bones of some three hundred of the first royal troops ever sent to India. Twenty-six soldiers were sent on shore, 'most of them not being able to stand.' The chief of the Company's factory at Carwar at that time was Mr. John Harvey, who entertained Captain Hudson and all the gentlemen and ladies on board 'in a splendid manner.'

One may picture to one's self the pleasure with which they escaped for a time from the ship and its scurvy-stricken crew. To Mr. Harvey and the Company's officials they were welcome as bringing the latest news from England. They were able to tell of Marlborough's victory at Oudenarde, and the capture of Lille and Minorca, while Harvey was able to tell them of Captain Kidd's visit to Carwar twelve years before, and to show them where the freebooter had careened his ship. But Mr. John Harvey found other matter of interest in his visitors. There were few Englishwomen in India in those days, and the unexpected advent of a fresh young English girl aroused his susceptibilities to such an extent that he forgot to report to Bombay the arrival of the *Loyall Bliss*, for which, he, in due time, received a reprimand. He quickly made known to Captain Cooke that he had taken a very great liking to his eldest daughter.

Mistress Catherine Cooke, 'a most beautiful lady, not exceeding thirteen or fourteen years of age.' Cooke was a poor man, and had left two more daughters in England; so, as Mr. Harvey 'proffered to make great settlements provided the father and mother would consent to her marriage,' Mistress Catherine Cooke, 'to oblige her parents,' consented also. There was little time for delay, as the captain of the *Loyall Bliss* was impatient to be off. The Company's ship *Tankerville* was on the coast, bound southward, and it was desirable they should sail in company for mutual protection. So, on the 22nd October, the *Loyall Bliss* made sail for Bengal, where she safely arrived in due time, leaving behind the young bride at Carwar.

To the lookers-on the marriage was repugnant, and can hardly have been a happy one for the young girl, as Harvey was 'a deformed man and in years.' He had been long on the coast, and by diligent trading had acquired a little money; but he had other things to think of besides his private trade, as we find recorded at the time that 'the *rajah* of Carwar continues ill-natured.' By the end of 1710, he made up his mind to resign the Company's service, wind up his affairs, and go to England; so Mr. Robert Mence was appointed to succeed him at Carwar, and, in April, 1711, Harvey and his child-wife came to Bombay.

But to wind up trading transactions of many years' standing was necessarily a long business, and there was no necessity for hurry, as no ship could leave for England till after the monsoon. As always happened in those days, his own accounts were mixed up with those of the Company, and would require laborious disentanglement. Before leaving Carwar, he had leased to the Company his trading *grab*, the

Salamander, and had taken the precaution to pay himself out of the Company's treasure chest at Carwar. Before long, there was an order to the Carwar chief to recharge Mr. Harvey 402 *pagodas*, 17 *jett*, and 4 *pice* he had charged to the Company for the use of the *Salamander*, the account having been liquidated in Bombay; from which it would appear that he had been paid twice for his ship.

The accounts of those days must have been maddening affairs owing to the multiplicity of coinages. Pounds sterling, *pagodas*, *rupees*, *fanams*, *xeraphims*, *laris*, *juttals*, *matte*, *reis*, *rials*, *cruzadoes*, *sequins*, *pice*, *budgerooks*, and dollars of different values were all brought into the official accounts. In 1718, the confusion was increased by a tin coinage called *deccanees*.[1] The conversion of sums from one coinage to another, many of them of unstable value, must have been an everlasting trouble.[2] In August we find Harvey writing to the council to say that he had at Tellicherry a chest of pillar dollars weighing 289 lbs. 3 ozs. 10 dwts., which he requests may be paid into the Company's cash there, and in return a chest of dollars may be given him at Bombay.

His young wife doubtless assisted him in his complicated accounts, and gained some knowledge of local trade. It must have been a wonderful delight to her to escape from the dullness of Carwar and mix in the larger society of Bombay, and she must have realized with sadness the mistake she had made in marrying a deformed man old enough to be her grandfather, at the solicitation of her parents. She made, at this time, two acquaintances that were destined to have considerable influence on her future life. On the 5th August, the *Godolphin*, twenty-one days from Mocha, approached Bombay, but being unable to make the harbour before nightfall, anchored outside; a proceeding that would appear, even to a landsman, absolutely suicidal in the middle of the monsoon, but was probably due to fear of pirates.[3]

That night heavy weather came on, the ship's cable parted, and the *Godolphin* became a total wreck at the foot of Malabar Hill. Ap-

---

1. They were issued at the rate of sixty-five for a *rupee*; before long, their value was reduced to seventy-two for a *rupee*, at which price they were much in request, and the governor reported that he expected to coin sixteen tons of them yearly.
2. In October, 1713, the Bombay Council decided that the *xeraphims*, being much debased with copper and other alloy, their recognized value should in future be half a *rupee*, or two *laris* and forty *reis*. The *xeraphim* was a Goa coin, originally worth less than one and sixpence. The name, according to Yule, was a corruption of the Arabic *ashrafi*.
3. The year before, the *Godolphin* had escaped from an Angrian fleet, after a two days' encounter within sight of Bombay.

parently, all the Englishmen on board were saved, among them the second supercargo, a young man named Thomas Chown, who lost all his possessions. There was also in Bombay, at the time, a young factor, William Gyfford, who had come to India, six years before, as a writer, at the age of seventeen. We shall hear of both of them again.

In October, came news of the death of Mr. Robert Mence at Carwar. 'Tho his time there was so small wee find he had misapplyed 1700 and odd pagodas to his own use,' the Bombay Council reported to the directors in London. In his place was appointed Mr. Miles Fleetwood, who was then in Bombay awaiting a passage to the Persian Gulf where he had been appointed a factor. With him returned to Carwar, Harvey and his wife, to adjust some depending accounts with the country people there.

We get an account of Carwar thirty years before this, from Alexander Hamilton, which shows that there was plenty of sport near at hand for those who were inclined for it, and it is interesting to find that the Englishmen who now travel in search of big game had their predecessors in those days—

> This country is so famous for hunting, that two gentlemen of distinction, *viz*: Mr. Lembourg of the House of Lembourg in Germany, and Mr. Goring, a son of my Lord Goring's in England, went *incognito* in one of the East India Company's ships, for India. They left letters directed for their relations, in the hands of a friend of theirs, to be delivered two or three months after their departure, so that letters of credit followed them by the next year's shipping, with orders from the East India Company to the chiefs of the factories, wherever they should happen to come, to treat them according to their quality. They spent three years at Carwar, *viz:* from *anno* 1678 to 1681, then being tired with that sort of pleasure, they both took passage on board a Company's ship for England, but Mr. Goring died four days after the ship's departure from Carwar, and lies buried on the island of *St. Mary*, about four leagues from the shore, off Batacola, and Mr. Lembourg returned safe to England.

Four months after his return to Carwar, Harvey died, leaving his girl-wife a widow. She remained at Carwar, engaged in winding up the trading affairs of her late husband, and asserting her claim to his estate, which had been taken possession of by the Company's officials, according to custom. According to the practice of the day, every merchant and factor had private trading accounts which were mixed up with the Company's accounts, so that on retirement they were not allowed to leave the country till the Company's claims were settled. In case of death, their estates were taken possession of for the same reason. Two months later, Mr. Thomas Chown, the late supercargo of the *Godolphin*, was sent down to Carwar as a factor, and, a few weeks after his arrival, he married the young widow.

Application was now made to the council at Bombay for the effects of her late husband to be made over to her, and orders were sent to Carwar for the late Mr. Harvey's effects to be sold, and one-third of the estate to be paid to Mrs. Chown, provided Harvey had died intestate. The Carwar factory chief replied that the effects had realized 13,146 *rupees* 1 *fanam* and 12 *budgerooks*; that Harvey had left a will dated the 8th April, 1708, and that therefore nothing had been paid to Mrs. Chown. It was necessary for Chown and his wife to go to Bombay and prosecute their claims in person. The short voyage was destined to be an eventful one.

On the 3rd November (1712), Chown and his wife left Carwar in the *Anne* ketch, having a cargo of pepper and wax on board, to urge their claim to the late Mr. Harvey's estate. The coast swarmed with pirate craft, among which those of Conajee Angria were the most numerous and the most formidable. It was usual, therefore, for every cargo of any value to be convoyed by an armed vessel. To protect the *Anne*, Governor Aislabie's armed yacht had been sent down, and a small frigate, the *Defiance*,[4] was also with them. The day after leaving Carwar they were swooped down upon by four of Angria's ships, and a hot action ensued.

The brunt of it fell on the governor's yacht, which had both masts shot away and was forced to surrender. The *ketch* tried to escape back to Carwar, but was laid aboard by two *grabs*, and had to surrender when she had expended most of her ammunition. In the action, Chown had his arm torn off by a cannon-shot, and expired in his wife's arms. So again, in little more than three years from her first marriage, Mrs. Chown was left a widow when she could hardly have been eighteen. The captured vessels and the prisoners were carried off; the crews to Gheriah and the European prisoners to Colaba. To make matters

---

4. The records are silent as to the *Defiance*, but it is mentioned by Downing, who says that, instead of doing his duty, the captain made the best of his way to Bombay. The story seems to be borne out by a faded letter from the captain to the directors, appealing against dismissal from the service.

worse for the poor widow, she was expecting the birth of an infant.

Great was the excitement in Bombay when the news of Mrs. Chown's capture arrived. The governor was away at Surat, and all that could be done was to address Angria; so a letter was written to him 'in English and Gentues,' asking for the captives and all papers to be restored, and some medicine was sent for the wounded. Just at this time also news was received of the Indiaman *New George* having been taken by the French near Don Mascharenas.[5] Sir John Gayer, who was on board, finished his troubled career in the East by being killed in the action.

After keeping them a month in captivity Angria sent back his prisoners, except the captains and mates and Mrs. Chown, whom he kept for ransom. In acknowledgment of kindness shown to the released prisoners by the *Seedee*, that chief was presented with a pair of Musquetoons, a fowling-piece, and five yards of 'embost' cloth. But in the governor's absence the council could do nothing about payment of ransom. When he returned, negotiations went on through the European prisoners in Colaba. Angria being sincerely anxious for peace with the English while he was in arms against his own chief, terms were arranged, and Lieutenant Mackintosh was despatched to Colaba with *Rs.*30,000 as ransom for the Europeans, and the sealed convention.

On the 22nd February (1713), he returned, bringing with him Mrs. Chown and the other captives, the captured goods, and the *Anne ketch*, but the yacht was too badly damaged to put to sea. According to Downing, Mrs. Chown was in such a state that Mackintosh, 'was obliged to wrap his clothes about her to cover her nakedness.' But her courage had never forsaken her; 'she most courageously withstood all Angria's base usage, and endured his insults beyond expectation.' Shortly afterwards she was delivered of a son. Out of her first husband's estate one thousand *rupees* were granted her for present necessities, with an allowance of one hundred *xeraphims* a month.

Very shortly afterwards we find her being married for the third time, to young William Gyfford, with the governor's approval. According to the statute law of Bombay, no marriage was binding, except it had the governor's consent; Hamilton tells us how on one occasion a factor, Mr. Solomon Loyd, having married a young lady without the

---

5. The name is now given to the group of islands to which Bourbon and Mauritius belong. At that time it generally applied to Bourbon, and especially to St. Paul's Bay, which was a favourite place of call for ships to water at.

governor's consent, Sir John Gayer dissolved the marriage, and married the lady again to his own son.

In October, two years and a half after her first husband's death, seven thousand four hundred and ninety-two *rupees*, being one-third of his estate, were paid over to her. It is carefully recorded that neither of her deceased husbands had left wills, though the existence of Harvey's will had been very precisely recorded by the council, fifteen months before. Young Gyfford, who was then twenty-five, appears to have been a favourite with the governor, and had lately been given charge of the Bombay Market. Eighteen months after his marriage, we find William Gyfford appointed supercargo of the *Catherine*, trading to Mocha. The office was a most desirable one for a young factor. It afforded him opportunities for private trade at first hand, instead of through agents, that in the mind of an adventurous young man quite outbalanced the perils of the sea.

In spite of small salaries, a goodly appearance was made by the Company's servants in public. At the public table, where they sat in order of seniority, all dishes, plates, and drinking-cups were of pure silver or fine china. English, Portuguese, and Indian cooks were employed, so that every taste might be suited. Before and after meals silver basins were taken round for each person to wash his hands. *Arrack*, Shiraz wine, and 'pale punch,' a compound of brandy, rose-water, lime-juice, and sugar, were drunk, and, at times, we hear of Canary wine. In 1717, Boone abolished the public table, and diet money was given in its place. Boone reported to the directors that, by the change, a saving of nearly *Rs.*16,000 a year was effected, and the Company's servants better satisfied.

On festival days the governor would invite the whole factory to a picnic in some garden outside the city. On such an occasion, a procession was formed, headed by the governor and his lady, in *palanquins*. Two large ensigns were carried before them, followed by a number of led horses in gorgeous trappings of velvet and silver. Following the governor came the captain of the *peons* on horseback, with forty or fifty armed men on foot. Next followed the members of the council, the merchants, factors, and writers, in order of seniority, in fine bullock coaches or riding on horses, all maintained at the Company's expense.

At the Dewallee festival every servant of the Company, from the governor to the youngest writer, received a '*peshcush*' from the brokers and bunyas, which to the younger men were of much importance;

as they depended on these gifts to procure their annual supply of clothes.

Of the country, away from the coast, they were profoundly ignorant. The far-off King of 'Dilly' was little more than a name to them, and they were more concerned in the doings of petty potentates with strange names, such as the Zamorin, the Zammelook, the Kempsant, and the Sow Rajah, who have long disappeared. They talked of the people as Gentoos, Moors, Mallwans, Sanganians, Gennims, Warrels, Coulis, Patanners, etc., and the number of political, racial, religious, and linguistic divisions presented to their view must have been especially puzzling. Owing to the numerous languages necessary to carry on trade on the Malabar coast, they were forced to depend almost entirely on untrustworthy Portuguese interpreters. Their difficulties in this respect are dwelt on by Hamilton—

> One great misfortune that attends us European travellers in India is, the want of knowledge of their languages, and they being so numerous, that one intire century would be too short a time to learn them all: I could not find one in ten thousand that could speak intelligible English, though along the sea coast the Portuguese have left a vestige of their language, though much corrupted, yet it is the language that most Europeans learn first, to qualify them for a general converse with one another, as well as with the different inhabitants of India.

After two years' work, as supercargo, on different ships, Gyfford was sent down to Anjengo as chief of the factory. Anjengo was at that time one of the most important factories on the Malabar coast, though of comparatively recent establishment. It was first frequented by the Portuguese, who, after a time, were ousted by the Dutch. It belonged to the *rani* of Attinga, who owned a small principality extending along sixty miles of coast. In 1688,[6] Rani Ashure invited the English to form a trading settlement in her dominions, and two were formed, at Vittoor (Returah) and Villanjuen (Brinjone). But for some reason, she became dissatisfied with the English, and the hostility of the Dutch,

---

6. According to some accounts, the first settlement was a few years earlier, but the dates of the early travellers are very unreliable. Hamilton says that a present was sent in 1685 to the queen; "A beautiful young English gentleman had the honour to present it to Her black Majesty; and as soon as the queen saw him, she fell in love with him, and next day made proposals of marriage to him, but he modestly refused so great an honour however, to please Her Majesty, he staid at court a month or two and satisfied her so well that when he left her court she made him some presents."

in spite of the alliance between the two countries in Europe, caused great trouble.

In November, 1693, John Brabourne was sent to Attinga, where, by his successful diplomacy, the sandy spit of Anjengo was granted to the English, as a site for a fort, together with the monopoly of the pepper trade of Attinga. Soon, the Dutch protests and intrigues aroused the *rani's* suspicions. She ordered Brabourne to stop his building. Finding him deaf to her orders, she first tried to starve out the English by cutting off supplies, but as the sea was open, the land blockade proved ineffectual. She then sent an armed force against Brabourne, which was speedily put to flight, and terms of peace were arranged. The fort was completed, and a most flourishing trade in pepper and cotton cloth speedily grew up. Anjengo became the first port of call for outward-bound ships.

The Anjengo fortification appeared so formidable to the Dutch, that they closed their factories at Cochin, Quilon, and Cannanore.[7] About 1700, Rani Ashure died, and the little principality fell into disorder. It was a tradition that only women should reign, and Ashure's successor was unable to make her authority felt. The Poolas, who governed the four districts into which the principality was divided, intrigued for power against each other, and before long the *rani* became a puppet in the hands of Poola Venjamutta. In 1704, a new governor, Sir Nicholas Waite, was appointed to Bombay. For some reason he left Brabourne without instructions or money for investment.[8] Their small salaries and their private trading seem to have made the Company's servants very independent. We constantly find them throwing up the service and going away, without waiting for permission. Brabourne went off to Madras, after delivering over the fort to Mr. Simon Cowse, who had long resided there, apparently as a private merchant, and who proved, as times went, a good servant to the Company.

The Company's service in those days was full of intrigue and personal quarrels. The merchant second in rank at Anjengo, John Kyffin, intrigued against Cowse so successfully, that Cowse was deposed, and Kyffin was made chief of the settlement. He appears to have been a thoroughly unscrupulous man. To enrich himself in his private pepper trade 'he stuck at nothing.' He took part in the local intrigues of

---

7. Bruce.
8. This is the reason given by Bruce for Brabourne leaving Anjengo, but the death of Brabourne's wife, in 1704, probably had a good deal to do with his leaving the place. Her tomb still exists.

Attinga, from which his predecessors had held aloof, played into the hands of Poola Venjamutta, quarrelled with the other local officials, and behaved with great violence whenever there was the slightest hitch in his trade. Kyffin's want of loyalty to the Company was still more clearly shown by his friendly dealings with their rivals, a proceeding that was strictly forbidden.

In June, 1717, Kyffin made known to the council at Bombay his wish to retire, and William Gyfford was appointed to succeed him as soon as the monsoon would permit. So, in due course of time, Gyfford and his wife went to Anjengo; but, in spite of his resignation, Kyffin stuck to his office, and evidently viewed Gyfford with unfriendly eyes. In the following April, intelligence reached the council at Bombay that Kyffin had had dealings with the Ostenders, and had been 'very assisting' to them; so, a peremptory order went down from Bombay, dismissing him from the Company's service, if the report of his assisting the Ostenders was true. If the report was not true, no change was to be made. A commission to Gyfford to assume the chiefship was sent at the same time. Interlopers and Ostenders, he was told, were not to receive even provisions or water. So Kyffin departed, and Gyfford reigned at Anjengo in his stead.

But the follies of Kyffin had roused a feeling against the English that was not likely to be allayed by Gyfford, who exceeded Kyffin in dishonesty and imprudence. He threw himself into the pepper trade, using the Company's money for his own purposes, and joined hands with the Portuguese interpreter, Ignatio Malheiros, who appears to have been a consummate rogue. Before long, religious feeling was aroused by the interpreter obtaining possession of some pagoda land in a money-lending transaction. Gyfford also aroused resentment, by trying to cheat the native traders over the price of pepper, by showing fictitious entries in the factory books, and by the use of false weights. The only thing wanting for an explosion was the alienation of the Mahommedan section, which, before long, was produced by chance and by Gyfford's folly.

It happened that some Mahommedan traders came to the fort to transact business with Cowse, who had resumed business as a private merchant; but he was not at leisure, so they went to the interpreter's house, to sit down and wait. While there, the interpreter's 'strumpet' threw some *hooli* powder on one of the merchants. Stung by the insult, the man drew his sword, wounded the woman, and would have killed her, if he and his companions had not been disarmed. Gyfford, when they were brought before him, allowed himself to be influenced by the interpreter, and ordered them to be turned out of the fort, after their swords had been insultingly broken over their heads. The people of Attinga flew to arms, and threatened the fort. For some months there were constant skirmishes. The English had no difficulty in defeating all attacks, but, none the less, trade was brought to a standstill; so Mr. Walter Brown was sent down from Bombay to put matters straight. Poola Venjamutta, who had all the time kept himself in the background, was quite ready to help an accommodation, as open force had proved useless.

Things having quieted down, Gyfford, 'flushed with the hopes of having peace and pepper,' devoted himself to trade. He had at this time a *brigantine* called the *Thomas*, commanded by his wife's brother, Thomas Cooke, doing his private trade along the coast. The year 1720 passed quietly. Force having proved unavailing, the Attinga people dissembled their anger, and waited for an opportunity to revenge themselves. So well was the popular feeling against the English concealed, that Cowse, with his long experience and knowledge of the language, had no suspicions.

There had been an old custom, since the establishment of the factory, of giving presents yearly to the *rani*, in the name of the Company; but for some years the practice had fallen into abeyance. Gyfford, wishing to ingratiate himself with the authorities, resolved on reviving the custom, and to do so in the most ceremonious way, by going himself with the presents for seven years. Accordingly, on the 11th April, 1721, accompanied by all the merchants and factors, and taking all his best men, about one hundred and twenty in number, and the same number of *coolies*, Gyfford started for Attinga, four miles up the river. Here they were received by an enormous crowd of people, who gave them a friendly reception. The details of what followed are imperfectly recorded, and much is left to conjecture, but Gyfford's foolish over-confidence is sufficiently apparent.

In spite of their brave display, his men carried no ammunition. Poola Venjamutta was not to be seen. They were told he was drunk, and they must wait till he was fit to receive them. He was apparently playing a double part, but the blame for what followed was afterwards laid on his rival, Poola Cadamon Pillay. Cowse's suspicions were aroused, and he advised an immediate return to Anjengo, but Gyfford refused to take the advice. He is said to have struck Cowse, and to have threatened with imprisonment. The *rani* also sent a message, advising a return to Anjengo. It was getting late, and to extricate himself from the crowd, Gyfford allowed the whole party to be inveigled into a small enclosure. To show his goodwill to the crowd, he ordered his men to fire a salvo, and then he found that the ammunition carried by the coolies had been secured, and they were defenceless. In this hopeless position, he managed to entrust a letter addressed to the storekeeper at Anjengo, to the hands of a friendly native. It reached Anjengo at one o'clock next day, and ran as follows:—

> Captain Sewell. We are treacherously dealt with here, therefore keep a very good lookout of any designs on you. Have a good look to your two trankers,[9] We hope to be with you tonight. Take care and don't frighten the women; we are in no great danger. Give the bearer a *chequeen*.[10]

But none of the English were to see Anjengo again. That night, or the next morning, a sudden attack was made, the crowd surged in on the soldiers, overwhelmed them, and cut them to pieces. The principal English were seized and reserved for a more cruel death. In the confusion, Cowse, who was a favourite among the natives, managed to disguise himself, got through the crowd, and sought to reach Anjengo by a little frequented path. By bad luck he was overtaken by a Mahommedan merchant who owed him money. Cowse offered to acquit him of the debt, but to no purpose. He was mercilessly killed, and thus the debt was settled. 'Stone dead hath no fellow,' as the chronicler of his death says. The rest of the English were tortured to death, Gyfford and the interpreter being reserved for the worst barbarities. Ignatio Malheiros was gradually dismembered, while Gyfford had his tongue torn out, was nailed to a log of wood, and sent floating down the river.

It is easy to picture to one's self the consternation in Anjengo, that 12th April, when, soon after midday, Gyfford's hasty note was received, and the same evening, when a score of wounded men (*topasses*) straggled in to confirm the worst fears; 'all miserably wounded, some with 12 or 13 cutts and arrows in their bodyes to a lower number, but none without any.' Gyfford had taken away all the able men with him, leaving in the fort only 'the dregs,' old men, boys, and pensioners, less than forty in number. At their head were Robert Sewell, who describes himself as storekeeper, captain and adjutant by order of Governor Boone; Lieutenant Peter Lapthorne, Ensign Thomas Davis, and

---

9. *Tranqueira* (Port.), a palisade.
10. Meaning sequin: the origin of the modern Anglo-Indianism, *chick*.

Gunner Samuel Ince.

The first three of them were absolutely useless, and Gunner Ince, whose name deserves to be remembered, was the only one of the four who rose to the situation. His first care was for the three English women, whose husbands had just been killed. By good fortune there happened to be in the road a small country ship that had brought a consignment of *cowries* from the Maldives. Mrs. Gyfford, for the third time a widow, Mrs. Cowse with four children, and Mrs. Burton with two, were hastily put on board, and sailed at once for Madras. No mention appears of Mrs. Gyfford having any children with her, but she carried off the factory records and papers, and what money she could lay her hands on.

She was no longer the confiding girl, who had given herself to Governor Harvey eleven years before. She had learned something of the world she lived in, and intended to take care of herself as well as she could. She even tried to carry off Peter Lapthorne with her, but Sewell intervened and prevented it. So giving him hasty directions to act as her agent, she passed through the dangerous Anjengo surf and got on board. A letter to her from Lapthorne, written a few weeks later, relates that the only property he could find belonging to her were 'two wiggs and a bolster and some ophium' in the warehouse.

Having got rid of the white women, Sewell and his companions set to work to hold the fort against the attack that was inevitable. From the old records we get an idea of what the fort was like. As designed by Brabourne, it covered a square of about sixty yards each way, but this did not include the two trankers, palisaded out-works, alluded to in Gyfford's note.

Ten years before, the attention of the council at Bombay had been drawn to the bad condition of the "Fort house, being no more then timber covered with palm leaves (*cajanns*) so very dangerous taking fire," and the chief of the factory was ordered to build "a small compact house of brick with a hall, and conveniencys for half a dozen Company's servants. And being advised that for want of a necessary house in the fort, they keep the fort gate open all night for the guard going out and in, which irregularity may prove of so pernicious consequence as the loss of that garrison, especially in a country where they are surrounded with such treacherous people as the natives and the Dutch," it was ordered that a "necessary house over the fort walls" should be built, and the gates kept locked after 8 o'clock at night.

How far these orders had been carried out does not appear; but the Company's goods were still kept in a warehouse outside the walls: some of the Company's servants also had houses outside, and the palm-leaf roofs were still there. For garrison they only had about thirty-five boys and pensioners, 'whereof not twenty fit to hold a firelock,' and, for want of a sufficient garrison, it was necessary to withdraw from the trankers, which were thought to be so important for the safety of the place. Desperate as was the outlook. Gunner Ince exerted himself like a man, animating everybody by his example. By his exertions, seven hundred bags of rice, with salt fish for a month, and the Company's treasure were got in from the warehouse, and an urgent appeal was sent to Calicut.

The surgeon had been killed with Gyfford; they had no smith or carpenter or tools, except a few hatchets, and the Attinga people swarming into Anjengo burned and plundered the settlement, forcing a crowd of women and children to take refuge in the small fort. Though no concerted attack was made at first, the assailants tried with fire arrows to set fire to the palm-leaf roofs, which had to be dismantled; and all through the siege, which lasted six months, the sufferings of the garrison were increased by the burning rays of a tropical sun or the torrential rains of the monsoon.

On the 25th April, they were cheered by the arrival of two small English ships from Cochin, where the intelligence of the disaster had reached; and received a small reinforcement of seven men with a consignment of provisions. A message of condolence also had come from the *rajah* of Quilon, who offered to receive the women and children, so one hundred and fifty native women and children, widows and orphans of the slain, were sent off. On the 1st May, an ensign and fifty-one men, collected by Mr. Adams from Calicut and Tellicherry, joined the garrison, and gave some relief from the constant sentry duty that was necessary. The enemy, meanwhile, had contented themselves with harassing the garrison by firing long shots at them; but it was rumoured that the *rajah* of Travancore was sending troops, and then they would have to sustain a serious attack.

Gunner Ince, on whom the whole weight of the defence rested, let it be known that in the last extremity he would blow up the magazine. It is cheering to find that there was at least one man who was prepared to do his duty. Sewell and Lapthorne got drunk, and joined with the warehouseman, a Portuguese named Rodriguez, in plundering the Company's warehouse and sending goods away to Quilon; the soldiers followed the example, and plundered the rooms inside the fort, while the late interpreter's family were allowed to send away, to Quilon, effects to the value of one hundred thousand *fanams*, though it was known that the Company had a claim on him for over two-thirds of the amount, on account of money advanced to him. Davis was dying of a lingering illness, to which he succumbed in the beginning of July.

On the 24th June, a vigorous attack was made on the fort from three sides at once. On one side the enemy had thrown up an entrenchment, and on the river side they had effected a lodgement in Cowse's house, a substantial building close to the wall of the fort. This would have soon made the fort untenable, so a small party was sent to dislodge the occupants. At first they were repulsed, but a second attempt was successful. Marching up to the windows, 'where they were as thick as bees,' they threw hand grenades into the house, which was hurriedly evacuated; numbers of the enemy leaping into the river, where some of them were drowned. Ince then bombarded them out of the entrenchment, and the attack came to an end. Several of the garrison were wounded, but none killed; but what chiefly mortified them was that the arms of the men slain with Gyfford were used against them.

After this the land blockade lingered on, but no very serious attack seems to have been made. A second reinforcement of thirty men was sent down by Adams from Calicut, and the *rani* and Poola Venjamutta sent 'refreshments,' and promised that the attacks of their rebellious subjects should cease. The *rani* also wrote to the Madras Council, and sent a deputation of one hundred Brahmins to Tellicherry, to express her horror of the barbarities committed by her people, and her willingness to join the Company's forces in punishing the guilty.

Intelligence of the disaster at Anjengo did not reach Bombay till the beginning of July. The monsoon was in full force, and no assistance could be sent till it was over. Men and supplies were gathered in from Carwar and Surat, and, on the 17th October, Mr. Midford, with three hundred men, reached Anjengo. His report on the state of affairs he found there makes it a matter of surprise that the place had not fallen. The safety of the fort had been entirely due to Gunner Ince. Sewell's behaviour was that of a fool or a madman. Together with Lapthorne, he had set the example of plundering the Company, and their men had done as much damage as the enemy.

Sewell, as storekeeper, had no books, and said he never had kept any. Lapthorne had retained two months' pay, due to the men killed with Gyfford, and asserted his right to it. Much of the Company's treasure was unaccounted for, and Mrs. Gyfford had carried off the books. Midford sent Sewell and Lapthorne under arrest to Bombay, where they were let off with a scolding, and proceeded to restore order. The *rani* and Venjamutta were friendly, but told him he must take his own vengeance on the Nairs for their inhuman action. So he commenced a series of raids into the surrounding country, which reduced it to some sort of subjection. Soon there came an order for most of his men to be sent back to Bombay, where warlike measures against Angria were on foot. A cessation of arms was patched up, and Midford installed himself as chief.

He proved to be no honester than his predecessors. He monopolized the pepper trade on his own private account, making himself advances out of the Company's treasury. In less than a year he was dead, but before his death Alexander Orme,[11] then a private merchant on the coast, was sent to Anjengo as chief of the factory, at the special request of the *rani*. Before long, Orme had to report to the council that there were due to the Company, from Gyfford's estate, 559,421 *fanams*, and that 140,260 gold *fanams* had disappeared during Midford's chiefship which could not be accounted for. Midford had also drawn pay for twenty European soldiers who did not exist. The council ascribed Midford's misdeeds to his 'unaccountable stupidity,' and the directors answered that 'the charges against Mr. Midford are very grievous ones.'

In September, 1722, the council received from Orme a copy of the treaty he had made with the *rani*. The following were the chief provisions. The ringleaders in the attack on Gyfford were to be punished and their estates confiscated; all Christians living between Edawa and Brinjone were to be brought under the Company's protection; the *rani* was to reimburse the Company for all expenses caused by the attack on Anjengo; the Company was to have exclusive right to the pepper trade, and were empowered to build factories in the *rani's* dominions wherever they pleased; the *rani* was to return all arms taken in the late outbreak, and to furnish timber to rebuild the church that had been burned. The treaty was guaranteed by the *rani's* brother, the *rajah* of Chinganatta. By the directors it was received with mixed feelings.

Last years letters took some notice about the affair at Anjengo, we had not then the account of the treaty Mr. Orme made with

---

11. The father of Robert Orme, the historian, who was born at Anjengo.

the queen of Attinga and king of Chinganetty, we are sorry to find it included in the treaty, that we must supply souldiers to carry on the war against her rebellious subjects for which she is to pay the charge, and in the interim to pawn lands for answering principal and interest, because it will certainly involve us in a trouble if we succeed, and more if we dont, add to this, the variable temper and poverty of those people may incline them to refuse to refund, and in time they may redemand and force back their lands. If the articles are fully complyed with they seem to be for the Companys benefit, but we fear we shall have the least share of it, to what purpose is her grant to us of all the pepper in her countrey, if our unfaithful people there get all for themselves and none for us, as you charge Mr. Midford with doing, we dont want an extent of lands, if we could but (obtain) pepper cheap and sufficient.

And what benefit will it be to us, to have the liberty of building factorys, which in event is only a liberty to lavish away our money, and turning quick stock into dead, unless you could be morally certain it would be worth while to get a small residence in the king of Chengenattys countrey, where it is said the Dutch make great investments of peice goods cheaper and better, than they used to do at Negapatam, and therefore have deserted it. We consider further, if such goods as are proper for our Europe market were procurable, how comes it we have had none hitherto, it is true we have had cloth from Anjengo good of the sorts, but invoiced so dear that we forbad sending more unless to be purchased at the prices we limited, since then we have heard no more about it, but we are told it is traded in to Bombay to some profit.

What profit will the putting the Christians between Edova and Brinjohn under our jurisdiction yeild to us, and what security can you have that the king of Chenganattys guarranteeship will answer and give full satisfaction. These are what appear to us worthy your serious and deliberate consideration to be well thought of before you come to a determination what orders to give. We find by your consultations in January 1722/23 you had sent down treasure to Anjengo, to enable the chief to levy souldiers to revenge the murder of the English, since you could not spare forces which as there exprest is absolutely necessary, for else the natives will have but contemptible thoughts of the

English, who will then loose their esteem. Had we ever found a benefit by their esteem, something might be said for it, but in the present case we fear we shall buy our esteem at too dear a rate, we should be extreamly glad to be mistaken and to find in effect what your 120th paragraph says in words, that you hope to make it a valuable settlement.[12]

We left Mrs. Gyfford flying from Anjengo in a small country ship, with two other English women and six children. The misery that the three poor widows must have endured for a month, crowded into a small country boat, without preparation or ordinary comforts, at the hottest time of the year, must have been extreme. On the 17th May, the fugitives landed at Madras. The council there granted them a compassionate allowance, of which Mrs. Gyfford refused to avail herself. After a time she made her way to Calcutta and joined her father's family, leaving, with an agent in Madras, the Anjengo factory books, which, after repeated demands, were surrendered to the Madras Council.

From Madras to Calcutta she was pursued by the demands of the Bombay Council. The books had been restored at Madras, and the Bengal government extracted Rs.7312 from her; but, in reply to further demands, she would only answer that she was 'an unfortunate widow, struggling with adversity, whose husband had met his death serving our Honourable Masters,' and that it was shameful to demand money from her, when she herself was owed large sums by the Company. She could only refer them to her agents at Madras and Anjengo. Still, she was in a considerable dilemma, as she could not get out of the country without a full settlement of accounts, and, if resistance was carried too far, her father might be made to suffer.

At this juncture an unexpected way of escape presented itself. Twelve months before this, Commodore Matthews had arrived in Bombay with a squadron of the Royal Navy for the suppression of piracy. But Matthews was more bent on enriching himself by trade than on harrying pirates; and, as his own trading was inimical to the Company's interests and certain to set the Company's servants against him, he had from the first assumed a position of hostility to the Company. Every opportunity was seized of damaging the Company's interests and lowering the Company's authority.

All who were in the Company's bad books found a patron and protector in Matthews; so, when in September, 1722, the flagship ap-

---

12. Letter from Court of Directors to Bombay, 25th March, 1724.

peared in the Hooghly, Mrs. Gyfford was quick to grasp the opportunity, that presented itself, of bidding defiance to her pursuers. She at once opened communication with Matthews, and besought his protection. She was an unfortunate widow who had lost two husbands by violent deaths in the Company's service, and, now that she was unprotected, the Company was trying to wring from her the little money she had brought away from Anjengo, while she herself had large claims against the Company.

This was quite enough for Matthews. Here was a young and pretty woman with a good sum of money, shamefully persecuted by the Company, to which he felt nothing but hostility. At one stroke he could gratify his dislike of the Company and succour a badly treated young woman, whose hard fate should arouse sympathy in every generous mind; so the Bengal council were told that Mrs. Gyfford was now under the protection of the crown, and was not to be molested.

In the hope of securing some portion of the money due to the Company, the council attached the *brigantine Thomas*, commanded by Mrs. Gyfford's brother. A letter was at once forthcoming from Matthews to say that he had purchased Mrs. Gyfford's interest in the vessel. Finding themselves thus forestalled, the council begged Matthews not to take her away from Calcutta till she had furnished security for the Company's claim of *Rs.*50,000, Matthews replied that he should take her to Bombay, where she would answer anything that might be alleged against her. As soon as he had completed his trading in Bengal, Mrs. Gyfford, with her effects, embarked on board the *Lyon*, and so returned to Bombay.

There, in January, 1723, we find her living under Matthews' roof, much to the wrath of the council and the scandal of her former acquaintances. By this time, the council had received from Anjengo more precise details as to what was due to the Company from Gyfford's estate. All the *cowries*, pepper, and cloth that were said to belong to Gyfford had been bought with the Company's money, and the Company's claim against his estate was nearly £9000. A stringent order was sent to Mrs. Gyfford, forbidding her to leave Bombay till the claim was settled. Matthews at once put her on board the *Lyon* again, and there she remained; not venturing to set foot on shore, lest the council should lay hands on her.

By the end of the year, Matthews was ready to return to England. Intent to the last on trade, he touched at Carwar, Tellicherry, and St. David's, and, in Mrs. Gyfford's interests, a visit was also paid Anjengo, to try and recover some of the property she claimed to have left there. She was not going to be put off with Lapthorne's 'two wiggs and a bolster.' In July (1724) the *Lyon* reached Portsmouth, and was put out of commission.

At first the directors appear to have paid little attention to Mrs. Gyfford, perhaps not thinking her worth powder and shot. Their principal anger was directed against Matthews, against whom they obtained a decree in the Court of Chancery for unlawful trading. But Mrs. Gyfford would not keep silence. Perhaps she really believed in the justice of her claims. She bombarded the directors with petitions, till at last, two years after her arrival in England, they tardily awoke to the fact that they themselves had substantial claims against her. They offered to submit the claims to arbitration, to which Mrs. Gyfford consented; but as she still refrained from coming to close quarters, they filed a suit against her in the Court of Chancery, nearly four years after her arrival in England.

Mrs. Gyfford promptly replied with a counter-suit, in which, among other things, she claimed £10,000 for presents taken by Gyfford to the *rani* of Attinga on that fatal 11th April, seven years before. Four years later, she was still deep in litigation, having quarrelled with her agent, Peter Lapthorne, among others. It is to be hoped, for her sake, that chancery suits were cheaper than they are now. Here we may say goodbye to her. For those who are curious in such matters, a search among the chancery records will probably reveal the result, but it is improbable that the Company reaped any benefit from their action. And so she passes from the scene, a curious example of the vicissitudes to which Englishwomen in India were exposed, two hundred years ago.

www.ingramcontent.com/pod-product-compliance
Lightning Source LLC
Chambersburg PA
CBHW021003090426
42738CB00007B/633